Animal
TRACKS & SIGNS

First published in North America in 2008 by the
National Geographic Society
1145 17th Street N.W.
Washington, D.C. 20036-4688

Copyright © 2008 Marshall Editions
A Marshall Edition
Conceived, edited, and designed by Marshall Editions
The Old Brewery, 6 Blundell Street, London N7 9BH, U.K.
www.quarto.com

Trade ISBN: 978-1-4263-0253-4
Library ISBN: 978-1-4263-0254-1

Library of Congress Cataloging-in-Publication Data available on request.

Originated in Hong Kong by Modern Age
Printed and bound in China by SNP Leefung Printers Limited

Publisher: Richard Green
Commissioning editor: Claudia Martin
Managing editor: Paul Docherty
Art director: Ivo Marloh
Picture manager: Veneta Bullen
Production: Nikki Ingram

Consultant: John A. Burton
Design and editorial: Tall Tree Ltd

For the National Geographic Society
Editor in Chief: Nancy Laties Feresten
Director of Design and Illustration: Bea Jackson
Assistant Editor: Priyanka Lamichhane

Founded in 1888, the National Geographic Society is one of the largest nonprofit scientific and educational organizations in the
world. It reaches more than 285 million people worldwide each month through its official journal, *National Geographic*, and its four
other magazines; the National Geographic Channel; television documentaries; radio programs; films; books; videos and DVDs; maps;
and interactive media. National Geographic has funded more than 8,000 scientific research projects and supports an education
program combating geographic illiteracy.

For more information, please call 1-800-NGS LINE (647-5463) or write to the following address:

NATIONAL GEOGRAPHIC SOCIETY
1145 17th Street N.W.
Washington, D.C. 20036-4688 U.S.A.

For information about bulk purchases, please contact National Geographic Books Special Sales: ngspecsales@ngs.org

For rights or permissions inquires, please contact National Geographic Books Subsidiary Rights: ngbookrights@ngs.org

Visit us online at www.nationalgeographic.com/books

Previous page A Bobcat runs through snow in Montana, United States.
This page and opposite Gray Wolves making tracks in snow, Minnesota, United States.
Following page A Dione Rat Snake, found from western Russia to Korea, emerges headfirst from its old skin.

Animal
TRACKS & SIGNS

BY JINNY JOHNSON
Editorial consultant: John A. Burton

NATIONAL GEOGRAPHIC

WASHINGTON, D.C.

CONTENTS

A Note on Names and Measurements

This book contains hundreds of images of particular species along with information about their tracks and other signs of their presence, but the information can very often be applied to their close relatives as well. For ease of understanding, the names of individual species have been capitalized. The measurement given for "Body" includes the head, unless otherwise stated. The illustrated tracks that accompany the information boxes on different animals are shown at approximately life-size, in black. In the natural world, measurements do vary greatly, and animals and their tracks and droppings may often be bigger or smaller than those shown. Where the track is either very small or too large to be completely shown, a scaled version has been included, in gray, so that its shape can be clearly seen.

Foreword

Wildlife films on television sometimes make it appear so very easy to spot wild animals. But if you go into a nature reserve or a local park, you will find it is often much more difficult to see them. Mammals, in particular, tend to be shy, and many come out only at night. But they do leave tracks and other signs, which you can learn to identify with a bit of practice.

By reading all the wonderful information in this book and looking at all the fascinating photos and drawings, you will be able to get an idea of the sheer variety of the tracks and trails left by animals, as well as all the other signs of their presence—the nests and dens they make, their droppings and pellets, which give us clues to what they have eaten, and the remains of the food itself. A huge amount of information can be gained about animals without seeing them in action.

Animals in action

And when you do want to see them in action, understanding their tracks and trails is often the best way of learning about the habits of shy and secretive animals. If you find a badgers' burrow, called a sett, you can follow the paths leading away from it to find out where the badgers like to go foraging. Then you can choose a comfortable tree to lean against or a stump to sit on and wait at dusk to see the badgers emerge. You may be able to follow them and watch them forage, as long as you keep your distance and remain very quiet. Around a stream or pond you might find tracks of animals such as deer, and this will help you choose a good place to hide and watch them next time they come to drink. Or you might find a heap of moth and beetle wings lying in a church porch, which lets you know that if you hang around on a warm summer's evening, there's a good chance you will see bats come in and hang upside down to eat their prey.

◀ *The photographer may have waited many days to take this shot of a Polar Bear and her cub.*

Tracking knowledge

Tracking expertise is essential for scientists, researchers, and filmmakers to carry out their work. Some trails are clear, such as those of hoofed animals. If you know which species live in an area, you can often work out what species made the tracks from their size and shape. Other trails are less clear, and an expert tracker needs vast skill and knowledge built up over many years to follow every trail. With the help of this book, you can start to learn these skills and put them to use, whether in your backyard, the beach, a local park, or a nature reserve.

Hope for the future

All over the world wildlife is disappearing, as forests are increasingly cleared and land is ploughed up for crops. But the more that people take an interest in wildlife, the more hope there is that places will be set aside where wildlife can live. So enjoy learning about all the different animals that are found in the various habitats, then go out into a nature reserve and see what you can find for yourself.

John A. Burton
CEO, The World Land Trust

Tracks and Footprints

When you walk on a soft surface, such as sand, mud, or snow, you leave behind footprints. Animals do just the same, and you can learn how to read their tracks. It's rare to find tracks that are clear and perfect like many of those in this book. You will often see partial tracks or tracks that have been walked over by another animal or otherwise damaged. When you find a track, first look at its shape. Notice how many toe or claw marks there are and whether there are marks of the pads on the underside of the foot.

Mammal tracks

There are several different kinds of mammal track—paws, cloven hooves, and non-cloven hooves. Some mammals walk on the soles of their feet like we do. Others, such as cats, walk on the tips of their toes.

▲ *This track, showing a palm pad, toes, and claws, has been made in mud by the front paw of a heavy Grizzly Bear.*

Black Bear

SOLE WALKERS
Plantigrade mammals, such as humans and bears, walk on the soles of their feet. They have five toes on each paw or foot, and many have claws; marks from the toe pads and claws usually appear in their tracks. There are one or more palm pads and a heel pad on each paw but these do not necessarily all show in tracks.

Horse

HOOF WALKERS
Animals such as horses, donkeys, and zebras have just one toe on each foot. The toe is covered in a tough casing called a hoof—a sort of toenail. The hoof leaves an almost circular track.

Lion

TOE WALKERS
Digitigrade mammals walk on their toes and most are fast runners. Their paws generally have a palm pad and four or five toes with pads. Most cats retract their claws into sheaths and so do not leave claw marks, but many other toe walkers, such as dogs and foxes, do. Some toe walkers have a dewclaw on the front feet and sometimes on the hind feet. This "extra" toe is higher up than the others and does not usually touch the ground.

CLOVEN-HOOF WALKERS Many hoofed animals, including deer and cattle, have four toes on each foot. They walk on the two middle toes. The outer toes, called dewclaws, are higher up the leg and are not used for walking. The dewclaws usually only show in tracks when the animal is walking on a very soft surface, such as deep snow. The two toes used for walking are covered with a tough hoof, or toenail, which is split, or cloven, into two parts called cleaves.

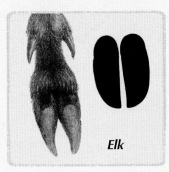

Elk

▲ *Even a very lightweight animal, such as this six-footed darkling beetle, will leave tracks if walking on soft sand.*

Other tracks

Amphibians and reptiles often leave tracks, too, and even snakes sometimes leave a trail of their wriggling movement. You may be able to tell what type of animal has left the track—such as a frog, newt, or tortoise—but it is usually very difficult to tell what species it is. Even insects can make footprints. Look in soft mud for the six-footed trail of the larger, heavier insects such as beetles.

Birds

Most birds have four toes on each foot. A few have only three toes, or the fourth toe may be higher up the leg and does not register in tracks. In most birds, three toes point forward and one back. Some, such as owls, can move the fourth toe backward, leaving tracks with two toes pointing forward and two backward.

▲ *These tracks were made by the three-toed feet of the Great Bustard.*

▲ *Kangaroos can reach speeds of 40 mph (60 km/h) by bounding along on their muscular hind legs.*

Types of Movement

Once you have learned to spot the tracks of different types of animals, you can start to look more closely and find out even more. By looking at the patterns of a track, the positions of the footprints, and the spaces between them, you may be able to work out how fast or slowly the animal was moving. Generally, the faster the animal is moving the more disturbance you'll see on the ground.

Animal gaits

The way an animal with legs moves is called its gait. The most common gaits are walking, trotting, galloping, and bounding or hopping. However, it's quite rare to find a long sequence of footprints in the wild, so you may want to start identifying gaits by looking at the tracks of domestic animals such as cats, dogs, and horses. You may be able to spot, for example, where a cat tracking its prey has started to move faster and changed from a slow walk to a gallop for the final pounce. Your best chance of finding gait patterns is after a fall of snow, when tracks register particularly clearly.

▲ *This Cheetah is galloping at full speed with all four feet off the ground.*

Gait Patterns

Walking

When an animal is walking, it lifts only one foot at a time. The stride (the distance between two tracks made by the same foot) will be small. The hind tracks will be close to the front tracks, perhaps even on top of them. In some animals, you may see marks of the body and tail dragging on the ground when the animal is moving slowly.

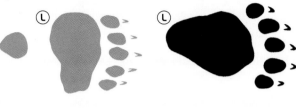

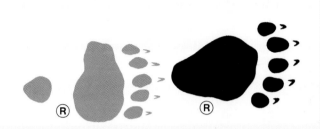

Bear tracks

Trotting

When an animal trots, it usually moves the front leg on one side at the same time as the hind leg on the other side—that is, the right front and left hind, and then the left front and right hind. The stride length is longer—there is a greater distance between tracks—and when an animal is trotting quickly, tracks may appear almost in a straight line.

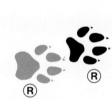

Wolf tracks

Galloping

A galloping or fast-running animal takes all four feet off the ground at one stage of the movement. The gait pattern shows groups of four tracks, with those of the hind feet appearing in front of those of the front feet. The animal takes off from its front feet and brings its hind legs up and forward, landing on the hind legs first.

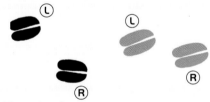

Deer tracks

Bounding/hopping

Like galloping animals, hopping animals have all four feet off the ground for a short period of the movement. Hopping animals, such as rabbits and hares, push off from the ground with the hind legs and then land with the hind feet slightly ahead of the front feet. You will see groups of four tracks, hind feet before the front.

Hare tracks

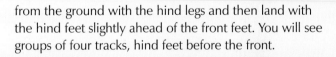

KEY TO TRACKS
🐾 *Front foot*   🐾 *Hind foot*   ℝ *Right foot*   ℒ *Left foot*

How to Track

Tracking an animal involves more than just finding a series of footprints on the ground. Tracks are one kind of evidence of an animal's presence, and an important one, but there are many other signs of activity to look for.

▲ *A Coyote feeds on the carcass of an Elk.*

Finding tracks

You are more likely to find tracks on soft surfaces. An animal's footprints rarely show on hard surfaces, such as rock, just as your footprints do not leave a mark on the pavement. Probably the easiest time to spot tracks is after a fall of snow. But remember that a print in snow appears much larger than the animal's actual foot. Otherwise, damp ground such as riverbanks, muddy paths, and sand are good places to look, particularly after rain. Tracks of the same animal will look different on different surfaces.

Droppings

After footprints, droppings are one of the most obvious animal signs. They show that an animal is in the area, perhaps marking its territory, and can tell us something about what it eats. Some birds also produce pellets (*see* pages 142–143), which are the indigestible parts of a bird's food, such as insect wings and fur. These reveal a great deal about the eating habits of the bird.

Feeding signs

You can find the evidence of animals' feeding habits all around you. Look for areas of cropped grass and stripped leaves or bark. The position of a feeding sign on a tree is a clue to the animal that made it (*see* pages 60–61). You may also find a carcass—the remains of a dead animal—although these are generally swiftly dealt with by scavengers and insects.

Nests and homes

Many people have seen molehills and entrance holes to rabbit warrens and there are lots of other signs of homes to look for. You may spy a bird's nest in a hedge or high in a tree, but if you do, never disturb it, or any other animal home. Or you may see an area of flattened grass and plants where an animal has been sleeping. A tree hole might be home to a bird or a squirrel.

▲ *These Elk scats, found in winter when Elk eat twigs, are firm; in summer, Elk eat moister food and the scats are softer.*

▲ *Blue Herons make their large nests high up in trees.*

Smaller creatures

It is not only large animals that leave signs of their activities. In any backyard or park you can see the shimmering trails left by snails, leaves chewed by caterpillars, spiders' webs, and earthworm casts (excreted soil). Get into the habit of looking closely at plants for signs of these miniature worlds.

▲ *Snow is a good surface in which to look for tracks. This enlarged wolf track clearly shows the paw's palm pad, four toes, and claws.*

Recording Tracks

When you go out tracking, always take a notebook and ruler with you so you can write down the measurements of tracks you find and make notes on other signs, such as marks on a tree or changes in a nest or burrow. When you find animal tracks, you will want to record what they look like, too, to identify them later or add to your collection. The best ways of doing this are by making a sketch of the track, photographing it, or making a plaster cast.

Sketching

Making a drawing of the track is simple and requires the least equipment. Make sure you measure the track carefully and note every detail. Drawing on graph paper is the easiest way to get everything in proportion.

▲ *When photographing a track, always make sure you put an object next to it to show scale, such as a coin or a camera lens cover, as shown here next to a wolf track.*

Measuring Tracks

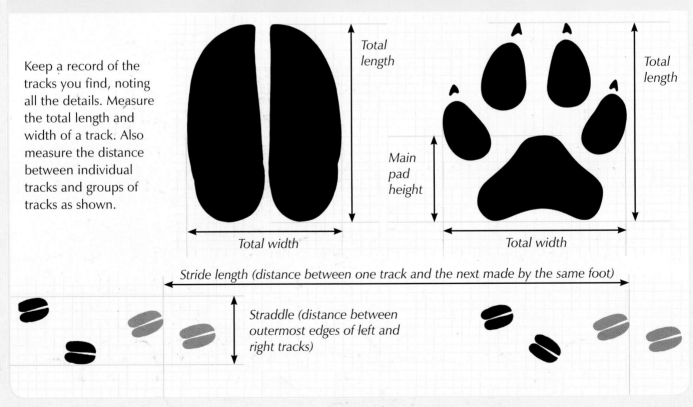

Keep a record of the tracks you find, noting all the details. Measure the total length and width of a track. Also measure the distance between individual tracks and groups of tracks as shown.

Total length

Total length

Main pad height

Total width

Total width

Stride length (distance between one track and the next made by the same foot)

Straddle (distance between outermost edges of left and right tracks)

Making Casts of Tracks

Making casts is a great way to record and collect your favorite animal tracks. You'll need to have some basic equipment with you and follow the simple steps below. The best casts are often made from tracks found in mud or fresh snow.

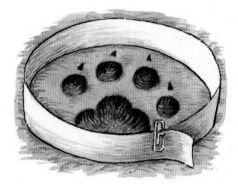

❶ You will need water, plaster of Paris, a mixing container, thin cardboard, paper clips, and a ruler. Also take a clean bag to wrap the cast in.

❷ Use a strip of cardboard to make a frame around your track, leaving about an inch all around. Push the card into the earth or snow and fix it with a paper clip or two.

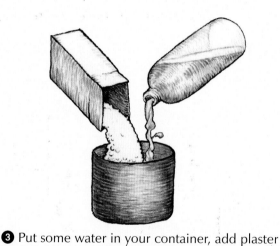

❸ Put some water in your container, add plaster of Paris, and mix. Add enough plaster to make a soft mixture about as thick as oatmeal.

❹ Pour the mixture into the frame to a depth of about an inch. Use the ruler to smooth the plaster into a flat surface. Leave the mixture to set for half an hour.

❺ Remove the frame, lift the cast carefully, wrap it, and take it home. Leave it to dry for a day. Clean it and, if you wish, paint it. Use a soft pencil to record on the bottom of the cast what animal made the track and when and where you made the cast.

Mammals

Mammals are warm-blooded animals with lungs for breathing air and a bony skeleton to support the body. Most have four legs and are covered in hair or fur. Many mammals are quite large, but that doesn't mean they are easy to spot in the wild. They are often active at night and secretive in their habits, making them difficult to find.

But each day most mammals must search for food, shelter, or mates, and they leave behind evidence of their activity, such as tracks. You can learn how to spot mammal tracks, look for signs of their dens and burrows, and identify their droppings. Look also for signs of feeding, such as chewed branches, stripped bark, and discarded fruit skins.

◀ *Brown Bears live in parts of North America, Europe, and Asia. In North America one type is known as the Grizzly Bear. At up to 1,700 lb (770 kg) in weight, they are one of the world's largest land-living carnivores and can be a scary sight up close.*

Big Cats

The big cats are among the largest flesh-eating mammals, and all are powerful hunters with sharp teeth and claws and excellent senses. They should be tracked only in the company of an experienced guide. You must be very careful not to get too close to a female with cubs. Lions live in groups, known as prides, but the other big cats are all normally solitary or live in small family groups of a mother and her cubs. Big cats are all suffering from habitat loss and hunting by humans.

▲ *Like other big cats, Lions scratch trees to keep their claws razor-sharp and to mark out their territory.*

Lion

▶ SCALE: ¼ *life-size*

▼ LIFE-SIZE *footprint of Lion*

SIZE Body: 8¼ ft (2.5 m); tail: 3¼ ft (1 m)
RANGE Africa south of the Sahara; Gir Forest, India (formerly more widespread in South Asia and North Africa)
HABITAT Savanna, open woodland, scrub
FOOD Large mammals, especially wildebeest, antelope, buffalo, and zebras, but will kill smaller prey, such as reptiles and even mice; also eats carrion
TRACKS AND SIGNS There is only one species of Lion. It is the largest of the African big cats and has distinctive tracks up to 5 in (13 cm) wide. Look for the large toe pads and two little indents on the back edge. Prints of the front feet are slightly larger than hind foot prints and the male's prints are bigger than the female's. The female's toes also leave smaller and narrower marks than the toes of the male.
COMMENTS Look for scrape marks on the ground and scratches on tree trunks where Lions have been sharpening their claws and marking their territory. These marks are a warning to other Lions to keep away but also let you know you're in Lion country.

Tracker Tips

Pug marks
The footprints of big cats are easily distinguished from those of other carnivores by their large size and lack of visible claw marks. Most cats have retractile claws, which can be, and usually are, pulled in. Tracks of front feet are known as "pug marks" and are larger than those of hind feet. Search for tracks in soft ground or along the banks of streams and rivers.

Scratching posts
Cats keep their claws sharp by scratching trees and posts, so look for these scratching posts. The marks are similar to those produced on a smaller scale by domestic cats.

Cheetah

SIZE Body: 4½ ft (1.4 m); tail: 31¼ in (80 cm)
RANGE Africa south of the Sahara; a few remote parts of west Asia; once found throughout Africa, southwest Asia, and India, except forested areas
HABITAT Grassland, semi-desert, scrub
FOOD Gazelle and other antelopes are its main prey; also eats the young of larger hoofed animals, as well as smaller mammals, such as hares, and birds
TRACKS AND SIGNS The Cheetah's track is about 3¼ in (8.5 cm) long and is instantly recognizable because it has claw marks. Unlike other big cats, the Cheetah cannot pull back, or retract, its claws into protective sheaths, so it leaves claw marks in its footprints. The claws help the Cheetah grip as it runs.
COMMENTS The Cheetah is the fastest runner of all the cats and the fastest sprinter of all land animals. It can run at speeds of up to about 70 mph (110 km/h) and is able to accelerate from a standing start to 40 mph (65 km/h) in three strides. Listen for its varied calls, which include chirps and purrs and a loud yelping call that can be heard as far as 1¼ miles (2 km) away.

Jaguar

SIZE Body: 6¼ ft (1.9 m); tail: 23½ in (60 cm)
RANGE Southern U.S.A., Central and South America, south to northern Argentina
HABITAT Tropical rain forest, savanna, scrub, usually near fresh water
FOOD Mammals such as peccaries, tapirs, and Capybaras; also preys on caimans and fish
TRACKS AND SIGNS This is the largest cat in South America; it has large paw prints, about 6 in (15 cm) wide, that are very similar to those of the Mountain Lion, but with a larger central pad. Jaguars live in deep remote forest and are rarely seen.
COMMENTS Has a variety of calls, including roars and a coughlike sound.

Small Cats

Besides the big cats (*see pages 18–19*) there are about 30 or so smaller species in the cat family. Like their larger relatives, small cats are expert hunters with sharp teeth and claws for attacking and killing prey. They move slowly and quietly as they track their food and may be very difficult to spot in the wild. Many small cats are active mostly at night and avoid humans. Look for their tracks and droppings—if you are lucky, you may hear their growls or yowling calls.

◄ *Lynxes live in high-altitude forests and grow a thick coat in winter to protect them from the cold.*

Serval

SIZE Body: 3¼ ft (1 m); tail: 14 in (35 cm)
RANGE Much of Africa but now extinct over much of the north
HABITAT Savanna, usually around river and stream banks with plenty of plant cover
FOOD Rats, mice, birds, frogs, and various insects, such as locusts
TRACKS AND SIGNS This solitary hunter leaves fairly small, rounded tracks about 2 in (5 cm) long. You will see droppings at intervals along the Serval's trail, and it makes only a few scratches, if any, to cover them.
COMMENTS The Serval generally hunts late in the day, around dusk. You may see it raising its head above long grass as it searches for birds and insects to catch.

Bobcat

SIZE Body: 3¼ ft (1 m); tail: 8 in (20 cm)
RANGE North America: southern Canada to Mexico
HABITAT Very adaptable, lives in forests, scrub, semi-desert, mountainous areas, even near towns
FOOD Rabbits, birds, larger prey such as deer
TRACKS AND SIGNS Footprints are rounded in shape and up to about 2 in (5 cm) long. As it walks, the Bobcat often places its back feet in the tracks of its front feet, but as it speeds up it leaves tracks of all four feet.
COMMENTS The Bobcat may also leave droppings along its tracks. It half-buries the droppings, so there will be scratch marks around them.

Tracking Pet Cats

Wild cats are not easy to see and track, so you may want to practice your skills by tracking pet cats in your neighborhood. Look for their paw prints on soft ground, such as flowerbeds, or in sand or mud. Like all cats from leopards to lynxes, the domestic cat's footprints are rounded, showing a central pad and four toe pads. Look for trails showing different types of movement. Tracks close together show that the animal was stalking slowly. A walking cat leaves more widely spaced tracks, and the trail of a jumping cat shows groups of four prints at varied intervals.

▼ *The domestic cat is a perfect animal on which to hone your tracking skills. Look for scratching signs on trees and fences and paw prints.*

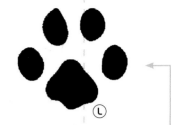

Eurasian Lynx

SIZE Body: 4¼ ft (1.3 m); tail: 10 in (25 cm)
RANGE Northern and eastern Europe; extinct in most of former range
HABITAT Coniferous forest, steppe
FOOD Small deer, hare, rodents, birds
TRACKS AND SIGNS There are several species of lynx and their tracks look similar to those of a domestic cat, but larger, at about 2¾ in (7 cm) long. When a lynx walks, its footprints appear almost in a single line.
COMMENTS The paws are covered with thick hair in winter to help the cat travel on snow. Claws may be visible in lynx tracks in the snow.

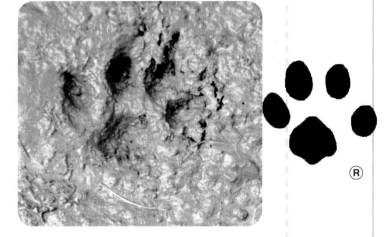

Stride length (between tracks made by the same foot) about 10 in (25 cm)

LIFE-SIZE tracks left by a walking domestic cat ▶

KEY TO TRACKS

🐾 *Front foot*
🐾 *Hind foot*
Ⓡ *Right foot*
Ⓛ *Left foot*

Dogs and Foxes

Most species of wild dogs and foxes are meat eaters, but some will eat insects and fruits. Many feed on almost anything they can find. They are fast runners with an excellent sense of smell and are less shy than cats, so are easier to track. They are dangerous, however, so never get too close or go near a mother with her young.

◄ *This Red Fox scat, or dropping, is dark and soft, which suggests that the fox may recently have eaten meat.*

Red Fox

SIZE Body: 3¼ ft (1 m); tail: 18 in (45 cm)
RANGE North America, Europe, northern Africa, western Asia; introduced in Australia
HABITAT Adaptable: desert, forest, Arctic tundra, grassland, urban areas near humans
FOOD A wide range, including rabbits, rats, insects, fruit, berries, human scraps
TRACKS AND SIGNS Although foxes have four toes on the back feet and five on the front, only four show on the front prints, so both tracks look very similar. At about 2 in (5 cm) in length, the front print is very slightly larger than the back. Fox prints are smaller than those of a similar-sized dog.
COMMENTS You have a good chance of tracking a fox in many areas—even if you live in a city. Look for twisted, sausage-shaped droppings along the trail or marking the animal's territory. Dens, which may have a strong musty smell, vary greatly, from simple holes beneath stones or tree roots, to uncovered holes in railway embankments, to more complex tunnels.

Hunting Dog

SIZE Body: 3½ ft (1.1 m); tail: 16 in (40 cm)
RANGE Originally many parts of Africa south of the Sahara, now only scattered areas
HABITAT Savanna, open woodland
FOOD Hares, rats, mice, larger animals such as gazelles and zebra
TRACKS AND SIGNS At about 3 in (8 cm) long, the tracks have a similar size and shape to those of a large domestic dog. The central pad is triangular, and the claws show clearly.
COMMENTS These dogs generally live and hunt in large packs of 20 or more adults and young. Listen for their different calls—the most common of these are the hooting sounds the dogs use to keep in touch with each other.

Arctic Fox

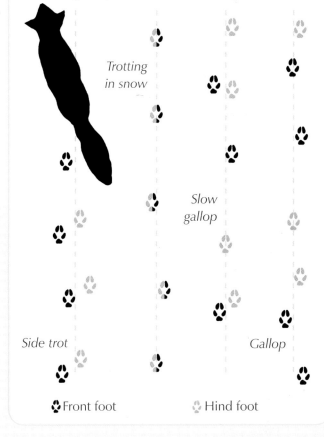

SIZE Body: 28 in (70 cm); tail: 16 in (40 cm)

RANGE Northern Europe, northern Asia, Alaska, northern Canada, Greenland, Iceland

HABITAT Tundra, coastal ice sheets, mountains

FOOD Lemmings and other small mammals, ground-nesting birds; will eat almost any creature, as well as food left by other predators, such as Polar Bears

TRACKS AND SIGNS The footprints of the Arctic Fox are quite small at only about 2 in (5 cm) in length, and the toes are set quite closely together. In winter, thick fur grows over the pads, so the prints are less clear than at other times of year. You may also spot marks left by the fox's tail in snow.

COMMENTS The Arctic Fox has a thick white coat in winter but a brownish one in summer, which helps it stay hidden in its surroundings. This fox tends to be nosy and may come quite close to have a look at humans encroaching on its territory.

How Fast?

A fox leaves different track patterns depending on where and how fast it is moving. When trotting in snow, the fox places its back feet in the tracks of the front feet. In a gallop the tracks are farther apart. If it turns its head while trotting on firm ground, the back feet swing away and the front feet swing in (a side trot).

Trotting in snow

Slow gallop

Side trot

Gallop

🐾 Front foot   🐾 Hind foot

Smelly Signals

Smell is all-important to members of the dog family, which leave their own scent trails as messages for each other. A fox may mark its territory by leaving piles of droppings where other animals will see them or by spraying urine onto trees and bushes. Another fox sniffing this can tell a great deal about the animal that left the mark and know whether to steer clear or not. Our noses are not so good—you may notice the strong smell left by a fox or a wild dog, but you will not be able to "read" its message like the animals can.

▶ *This fox is marking its territory by spraying urine on the grass.*

Wolves

Wolves and other members of the dog family are excellent runners and travel long distances as they chase prey or search for carrion. Most have a strong body, long legs, and a bushy tail. Males and females look alike, but the males are usually slightly larger. They are intelligent, social animals and often form groups to hunt prey larger than themselves. Watch for signs of pack activity, such as many tracks together, and listen for their calls as the animals keep in touch.

◀ *Coyote scat often contains a lot of easily visible hair from the animal's prey, in this case probably deer.*

Gray Wolf

SIZE Body: 5 ft (1.5 m); tail: 20 in (50 cm)
RANGE Northern North America, Asia, parts of southern and eastern Europe
HABITAT Tundra, open woodland, forest
FOOD Large mammals such as Moose, other deer, mountain sheep, beaver, carrion
TRACKS AND SIGNS Wolf tracks are like those of big domestic dogs but tend to be longer and wider. The front print is up to 4¼ in (11 cm).
COMMENTS Wolves have a wide range of calls, including whines, howls, yelps, and growls. The whole pack may howl together and the sound can be heard for miles.

Coyote

SIZE Body: 3¼ ft (1 m); tail: 16 in (40 cm)
RANGE North America: Canada to Central America
HABITAT Adaptable, living in grassland, forest, mountainous regions, and built-up areas
FOOD One of the fastest canids, will hunt jackrabbits, rodents, fish; groups of 2 or 3 also hunt much larger animals, including deer and sheep
TRACKS AND SIGNS At up to 2½ in (6 cm), the front footprints are a little larger than the hind ones; the claws on the two outside toes do not usually show up in prints made on harder ground.
COMMENTS Coyotes may be quite bold and investigate places such as campsites. Never go near the den of a mother and her pups, as she will then become anxious and want to move her young to a new safe place.

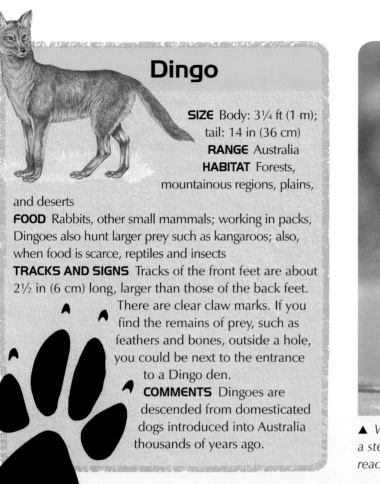

Dingo

SIZE Body: 3¼ ft (1 m);
tail: 14 in (36 cm)
RANGE Australia
HABITAT Forests,
mountainous regions, plains,
and deserts
FOOD Rabbits, other small mammals; working in packs,
Dingoes also hunt larger prey such as kangaroos; also,
when food is scarce, reptiles and insects
TRACKS AND SIGNS Tracks of the front feet are about
2½ in (6 cm) long, larger than those of the back feet.
There are clear claw marks. If you
find the remains of prey, such as
feathers and bones, outside a hole,
you could be next to the entrance
to a Dingo den.
COMMENTS Dingoes are
descended from domesticated
dogs introduced into Australia
thousands of years ago.

▲ *Wolves have great stamina and can cover many miles at
a steady trot of 6 mph (10 km/h). During a chase, they can
reach speeds of up to about 30 mph (50 km/h).*

Tall Tails

A wolf pack is always led by a male and female pair,
which are mates. They both carry their tails high to show
their position. Other wolves must not carry their tails as
high as the leaders, and low-ranking animals must keep
their tails well down.

A tail held straight out shows a wolf is about to attack or
hunt, while a drooping tail shows it is relaxed. When two
wolves meet, they sniff each other to find out which one
is dominant. The dominant wolf then raises his tail, while
the other keeps his between his legs.

A high tail means
a dominant wolf,
a pack leader.

A horizontal or stiff tail
tells us that this wolf is about to
attack or hunt.

A drooping tail
shows that this wolf
is relaxed.

A tucked-in tail
is a sign of a wolf's
submission.

Otters

Otters, like weasels and skunks, belong to the mustelid family of flesh-eating mammals. They are expert swimmers and catch nearly all their food in water. While swimming they can close off their nostrils and ears. An otter's fur is short and very thick. It keeps the skin dry by trapping a layer of air around the body. Otters are very playful and inquisitive.

◄ *Otter droppings, like these from a Eurasian Otter, contain fish scales and bones from fish, frogs, and small mammals.*

Eurasian Otter

SIZE Body: 35 in (90 cm); tail: 16 in (40 cm)
RANGE Europe, Asia, northern Africa
HABITAT Rivers, lakes, estuaries
FOOD Mainly fish, shellfish, frogs, birds; also rodents
TRACKS AND SIGNS The Eurasian Otter spends much of its time in the water, but when on land it leaves tracks up to 3 in (7 cm) in length that often show all five toes and claw marks. Otters tend to bound along, leaving widely spaced groups of footprints. Look for remains of fish and shellfish shells on riverbanks. Also look for piles of droppings, which are often left on stones or logs on the riverbank, where they advertise the animal's presence to others.
COMMENTS Otters usually dig burrows in the riverbank. Outside the burrow you may see bare spots on the ground where the otters roll and marks left when they slide down through mud or snow to the water.

Cape Clawless Otter

SIZE Body: 3 ft (95 cm); tail: 26 in (65 cm)
RANGE Africa south of the Sahara, except rain forests
HABITAT Streams, lakes, rocky coasts
FOOD Shellfish such as crabs; mollusks, including octopus, and frogs; also eats fish and worms
TRACKS AND SIGNS Its 4-in (10-cm) prints on muddy shores show five long toes on each foot. Close to the water, look for piles of droppings, which usually contain the remains of crabs.
COMMENTS The Clawless Otter has no claws. Its sensitive feet are just right for finding shellfish in muddy river bottoms and holding them as it feeds.

▲ *This Sea Otter is floating on its back while it eats a meal of abalone, a type of shellfish.*

Giant Otter

SIZE Body: 6 ft (1.8 m); tail: 26 in (65 cm)

RANGE Northern South America to Paraguay and northern Argentina

HABITAT Rivers and lakes in tropical rain forests

FOOD Fish is the main food, but also eats crabs, snakes, and even small caiman

TRACKS AND SIGNS This otter's large feet have thick webbing between each toe. Its tracks are similar to those of the Eurasian Otter but three to four times larger. Look for areas of riverbank cleared of plants, where Giant Otters like to lie and groom themselves.

COMMENTS The largest otter by length and the largest of the mustelid group of animals, this otter is now endangered. It is much noisier than other otters and makes loud screaming calls.

Signs of the Sea Otter

Sea Otters live in the ocean and spend much more time in water than other otters do, so it is rare to find their tracks on land. But if you are in the area where Sea Otters live—the rocky Pacific coastline of North America—you may be lucky enough to spot these wonderful creatures bobbing up and down in the waves. Look for their shiny black, whiskery noses among beds of seaweed floating on the water surface. And you might spot a Sea Otter feeding. The animal lies on its back with a rock on its chest, banging a clam or other shellfish against the rock until its hard shell is broken, before eating the soft flesh inside. Like other otters, Sea Otters are very playful and can be seen leaping and surfing in the waves.

Martens and Polecats

These animals belong to the mustelid or weasel family of flesh-eating mammals. Like their relatives, they are fast-moving hunters, with long, slim bodies, short legs, and furry tails. They eat a wide range of foods and will gobble up fruit, insects, and even honey if they haven't made a kill. They mark their territories with a smelly fluid from glands near the tail, so you might smell these creatures before you see them.

▲ *The American Marten is a strong climber. It spends much of its time in trees and is most active after daylight.*

European Polecat

SIZE Body: 18 in (46 cm); tail: 6 in (14 cm)
RANGE Europe; introduced to New Zealand and Morocco
HABITAT Forests, fields, woodland, marshes, farmland
FOOD Mice and other rodents, birds, frogs, fish, insects, and other small creatures
TRACKS AND SIGNS The tracks show five toes on each foot—the outer toe set well back—and long claw marks. Front prints are about 1½ in (3.5 cm) long, rear prints slightly longer. You may also see marks of the tail on soft surfaces such as snow. Polecats generally bound along, leaving a trail of groups of four prints. Their droppings are very strong-smelling but not usually left in obvious places.
COMMENTS European Polecats make dens in hollow trees or take over the burrows of other animals. You may also find signs of them living in sheds and other outbuildings. The domestic ferret is a close relative of polecats.

American Marten

SIZE Body: 18 in (45 cm); tail: 9 in (23 cm)
RANGE Northern and western North America
HABITAT Coniferous forest
FOOD Voles, mice and other small mammals, birds, insects, fruit, berries
TRACKS AND SIGNS The American Marten, or Pine Marten, has five toes on each foot, like other members of the weasel family, but often only four show in its tracks, which are 2½ in (6 cm) long. In winter, thick hair grows on its feet, and its tracks may be very blurred. Martens sometimes leap from tree to tree, leaving no trail on the ground.
COMMENTS This animal swims and climbs well and spends much of its time in trees. It dens in hollow trees, crevices, or vacant ground burrows. It is usually more active at night or in twilight hours than during the day.

Tayra

SIZE Body: 28 in (70 cm); tail: 18 in (45 cm)
RANGE Mexico, Central and South America
HABITAT Forest
FOOD Small mammals, birds, fruit
TRACKS AND SIGNS Like martens, polecats, and weasels, the Tayra belongs to the mustelid family. Its tracks are about 3 in (7.5 cm) wide and show five toes. The trail can be difficult to follow as Tayras may climb a tree then leap from branch to branch for a while before coming back down to the ground. Its tail may leave marks on the ground.
COMMENTS Tayras are strong climbers, so look for them in the trees above you. They make a barking call when scared.

Feeding Signs

Martens and polecats are fierce little hunters that will take almost any prey they can find. They also eat carrion—the remains of animals that are already dead and may have been killed by other hunters. A favorite food of polecats is frogs and toads. Look for remains of these prey on a riverbank. Polecats always leave the toads' heads uneaten because they contain poison glands.

▼ *A European Polecat keeps an eye out for prey on the forest floor. Polecats hunt voles, mice, and other small animals, usually at night.*

Carnivore Scats

The droppings of animals, called scats or dung, can tell the tracker a great deal, so it is a good idea to know something about them. The shape and size of animal scats can be quite distinctive and may tell you what sort of creatures are in the area and what they eat. Never handle any droppings you find because they can carry disease and parasites and could make you ill.

Identification

Scats containing fish scales are likely to be from aquatic species, such as mink or otters; scats containing fur and bones will be from land-based predators. Pet carnivores, such as dogs and cats, tend to produce scats quite unlike those of their wild relatives, because their diets often contain no fur, feathers, or bones. Carnivore scats are usually tube-shaped and sometimes pointed. They are generally brownish but some carnivores, such as bears, eat a surprising amount of berries and other fruit and this may alter the color. Many scats contain fur, feathers, and teeth and some have a white outer coating, which comes from digested bone.

▲ Latrine pits containing exposed dung, like the one above, are a sign that Eurasian Badgers are active in your area.

Territory marking and toilets

Some carnivores mark their territories by leaving scats in obvious places. Most carnivore scats have distinctive musky odors, which come from the smell of digested food remains and from special scent glands. These glands are also used to mark an animal's territory directly, and the scents are often used alongside dung and urine. Many carnivores dig special holes called latrine pits, in which they place their dung. Eurasian Badgers are well known for digging shared latrine pits well away from the setts or burrows where they live together. The solitary American Badger, in contrast, often buries its scats in a pile of earth outside its home.

▲ This otter is marking its territory by depositing its spraint, or dung, on top of a large rock.

Types of scats you might find

CAT FAMILY Domestic cat scat is sausage-shaped and up to 3 in (8 cm) long. Wild cat scats are a similar size but more twisted and lumpy and may contain bits of bone. Lynx scats are sausage-shaped, with one end pointed, and up to 10 in (25 cm) long. They may contain fur and feathers; if they contain bone, they may appear gray.

DOG FAMILY Dog scats are sausage-shaped, not twisted, and range widely in length. Fox scats are generally twisted with pointed ends and up to about 4 in (10 cm) long. They may be brownish or gray in color and contain fur, feathers, and bone as well as the remains of insects and fruit and berries. Fox scat has a very strong smell.

MUSTELIDS The scats of this large group vary greatly. Badger scat may be very loose and soft but is more often large and sausage-shaped with a rough surface. The scats contain plant remains as well as insect parts and fur. Polecat and weasel droppings are slender and very twisted, tapering to a pointed end. Polecat scat is about 2¾ in (7 cm) long, slightly larger than weasel scat. Marten scat is thicker but also has a tapering shape.

BEARS Bears produce large scats that are clumpy rather than sausage-shaped. They are generally brownish and contain both plant and animal remains.

Identify the Animal

Eight of these droppings were made by carnivores: polecat, weasel, badger, lynx, wild cat, bear, marten, and fox. Two of the droppings were left by plant eaters—try to identify which is which.

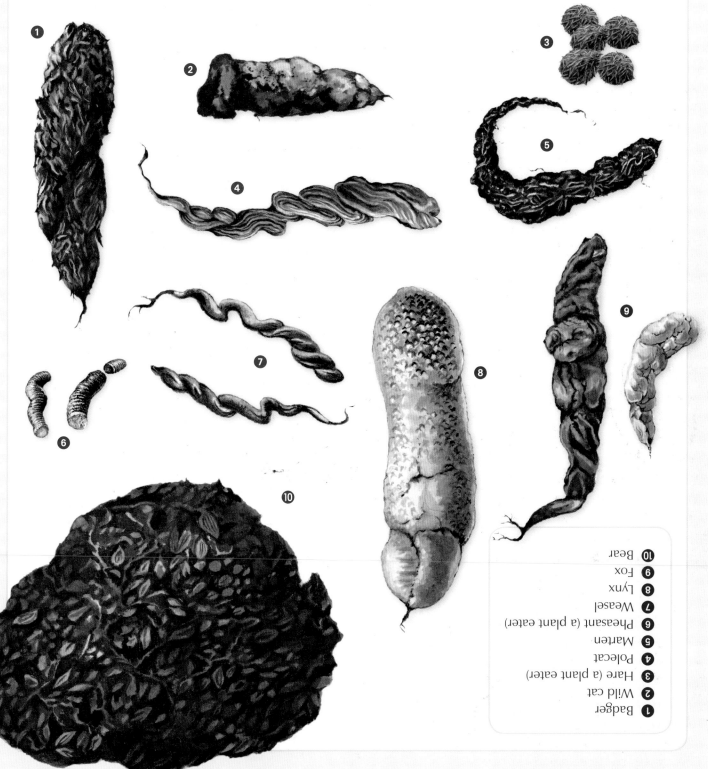

10 Bear
9 Fox
8 Lynx
7 Weasel
6 Pheasant (a plant eater)
5 Marten
4 Polecat
3 Hare (a plant eater)
2 Wild cat
1 Badger

Weasels, Mink, and Stoat

These members of the mustelid family are all agile meat-eaters with a long, supple body, a long tail, and short legs, with five toes on each foot. They eat mainly mice and other small rodents. They are inquisitive creatures whose trails are likely to show them constantly changing direction in search of food.

◄ *This Short-tailed Weasel, also called the Stoat or Ermine, is in its summer coat, with brown fur on its head, back, and tail.*

Short-tailed Weasel

SIZE Body: 12 in (30 cm); tail: 5 in (12 cm)
RANGE Northern Europe and Asia, North America; introduced in New Zealand
HABITAT From tundra to forest; likes places where there are plants or rocks among which to hide
FOOD Rats and mice, birds, eggs, frogs, and insects; sometimes attacks prey as large as hares
TRACKS AND SIGNS Unusual to see clear tracks as the Short-tailed Weasel is light in weight, has small hairy feet, and tends to jump rather than walk. A clear print will show five toes and claws and three central pads that may appear joined. A trail may show groups of four prints as the animal bounds along. Hind prints are 1½ in (3.5 cm) long. You may see tail marks too.
COMMENTS Keep a look out for droppings, which are twisted and sausage-shaped. The droppings contain the remains of fur, bones, and feathers.

American Mink

SIZE Body: 20 in (50 cm); tail: 8 in (20 cm)
RANGE North America; introduced in many parts of Europe and Asia
HABITAT Near streams and lakes
FOOD Fish, frogs, crayfish, baby turtles; also worms, insects, birds
TRACKS AND SIGNS The fifth inside toe is small and slightly below the others—it does not always show on tracks. Claw marks sometimes show. At about 2 in (5 cm) in length, the front feet are larger than the back. Look for mink dens in riverbanks, where the mink may dig its own burrow or use a Muskrat home after eating the owner. You may find scraps of fur around the entrance hole as well as fish bones, feathers, and eggshells.
COMMENTS The mink is a type of weasel with thick, silky fur. It is farmed for its fur, and escaped farmed mink now live wild in many parts of Europe.

A Rare Relative

The Black-footed Ferret, a slender mustelid and a close relative of the weasels, is now one of the rarest mammals in North America. It was once extremely common on prairie grasslands, where it preyed mostly on prairie dogs. The ferrets spent much of their lives in prairie dog burrows, where they slept and hunted. However, as large areas of grassland were made into farmland, huge numbers of prairie dogs were destroyed by habitat loss and poisoning. The Black-footed Ferret began to die out, as a family of four ferrets needs to eat about 250 prairie dogs a year. The ferrets are now being bred in captivity, and several hundred have already been released into the wild to build up new populations. Perhaps in the future it will be possible to find their tracks once again.

▲ *In 1986, only 50 Black-footed Ferrets were left alive, all in captivity. Their numbers have now stabilized at about 250 in captivity, with many others released into the wild.*

Least Weasel

SIZE Body: 8 in (20 cm); tail: 2 in (5 cm)
RANGE North America, Europe, North Africa, Asia; introduced in New Zealand
HABITAT Fields, open woodland, farmland
FOOD Mainly mice; also eats other small rodents
TRACKS AND SIGNS This is the smallest weasel and is very lightweight, so its tracks, about ½ in (1.5 cm) long, are not always clear. Also the soles of the feet are hairy, which may blur prints. The fifth (inside) toe does not always show in tracks. A galloping animal, it leaves groups of four prints with a gap of 12 in (30 cm) or more between them.
COMMENTS Least Weasels are small and slender enough to follow mice and other small rodents into their homes to prey on them. Look for the remains of Least Weasel prey left outside their holes and burrows.

What's the Difference?

There is little difference between a Short-tailed Weasel (also known as a Stoat or Ermine) and a Least Weasel—they are close relatives. The Short-tailed Weasel is slightly larger and has a black-tipped tail. The fur of both species turns white in the winter, but only in those animals that live in regions where snow often falls.

Badgers

Badgers belong to the same family as weasels. They are all strongly built animals, with sturdy bodies and short, strong legs. Their front legs are particularly powerful, with big claws for digging. Badgers also have sharp teeth. They are very adaptable, able to live in lots of different habitats, and eat many kinds of food. With their pointed faces and black-and-white markings, badgers may look appealing—but remember, they can be fierce, and those sharp claws and teeth can do a lot of damage.

American Badger

SIZE Body: 28 in (72 cm); tail: 6 in (15 cm)
RANGE Southwestern Canada to Mexico
HABITAT Open areas in woodland and forest
FOOD Ground squirrels, rats and mice, snakes, birds, roots, fruits, berries
TRACKS AND SIGNS Tracks are similar to those of the Eurasian Badger, with claw marks on the front feet.
COMMENTS Look out for signs of a badger's den, called a sett. The entrance is oval-shaped and there is often a mound of dug-out earth outside. In rattlesnake country you may see lots of snake rattles discarded near the den—snakes are a favorite food.

Eurasian Badger

SIZE Body: up to 35 in (90 cm); tail: 8 in (20 cm)
RANGE Europe, Asia
HABITAT Forest, woodland
FOOD Almost anything, including mice, birds, frogs, reptiles, insects, nuts, berries, seeds, carrion
TRACKS AND SIGNS Badgers are quite heavy, and often leave clear footprints about 2½ in (6 cm) long. The central pad and five toe pads can usually be seen, as well as marks of the long claws. The prints sometimes look to be slightly turned inward. Eurasian Badgers use shared dung pits, or latrines, which can be found near their setts.
COMMENTS When walking, the badger holds its body close to the ground, so you may see marks of its coarse fur. Look for badger latrines— these are shallow holes near the sett, where they leave their droppings.

Ratel or Honey Badger

SIZE Body: 30 in (75 cm); tail: 12 in (30 cm)
RANGE Africa south of the Sahara, Middle East, India
HABITAT Usually dry areas, but also lives in forest and grassland
FOOD Small mammals, birds, reptiles, insects; they are also very fond of honey and bee larvae
TRACKS AND SIGNS As well as claws, toes, and a central pad, the track often shows the pad behind the central pad (called the proximal pad). Sometimes only four of the five toes show in the footprint. The print of the front foot is about 3¼ in (8 cm) long; the back is about 1½ in (6.5 cm) long.
COMMENTS Empty dung beetle balls are a sign of Ratel activity. The Ratel bites the balls open to snack on the larvae inside.

Tracking Honey

The Ratel is also known as the Honey Badger because of its fondness for honey and bee larvae. In some parts of Africa, the Ratel itself becomes a tracker—it follows a bird called the Honeyguide, which feeds on bee larvae and beeswax and is never far from a hive. Once the bird has led the Ratel to a bees' hive, the mammal breaks the nest open with its big, sharp claws, and both creatures get a good meal.

▼ *These Eurasian Badgers are snug in the safety of their sett, which enables them to survive both hot and cold weather.*

Skunks and Wolverine

Skunks and the Wolverine belong to the mustelid group of meat-eating mammals. They hunt prey but will also eat berries and carrion. Skunks live in burrows; Wolverines den in caves or under trees. Wolverines are dangerous and should be avoided. Get too close to a skunk and you risk being exposed to its terrible smell!

▶ *A Wolverine takes a rest during a long journey. Although strong and fierce, it lopes along slowly in its search for prey.*

Striped Skunk

SIZE Body: 15 in (38 cm); tail: 15 in (38 cm)
RANGE North America: southern Canada to northern Mexico
HABITAT Woods, grassland, desert, city areas
FOOD Rats, mice, and other small mammals, insects, fruit, plant matter
TRACKS AND SIGNS It has five toes on each foot, and these and the claws generally show on prints. Front prints are about 1½ in (3.5 cm) long. Its trail tends to be irregular, and the faster the skunk is moving, the more likely the tracks are to show the hind feet overlapping the front ones.
COMMENTS The Striped Skunk is most active at night—listen for squeals, screeches, and low churring noises. If in danger, it may spray a foul-smelling scent.

Western Spotted Skunk

SIZE Body: 13 in (33 cm); tail: 11 in (28 cm)
RANGE Western North America to Central America
HABITAT Scrub, brush, rocky areas, urban areas
FOOD Plant matter and insects in summer; rats, mice, and other small creatures in winter
TRACKS AND SIGNS Similar to those of the Striped Skunk, but slightly smaller. All five toes and claws usually show, and track pattern tends to be irregular. Look for piles of small dark droppings, which are about ¾ in (2 cm) long.
COMMENTS Skunks can dig burrows, but they often use burrows that other animals have left. Keep an eye out for skunk dens made in sheds and other buildings.

Wolverine

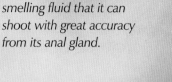

SIZE Body: 3¼ ft (1 m); tail: 10 in (25 cm)

RANGE Northern North America, parts of Scandinavia, northern Asia

HABITAT Tundra, forest

FOOD Lemmings and other small mammals, birds' eggs, berries, and carrion; sometimes catches larger mammals, such as sheep

TRACKS AND SIGNS The Wolverine's tracks are much larger than those of most other mustelids, and the front print is up to 7 in (18 cm) long. The animal has five toes on each foot, but sometimes only four show in the print. The trail of a Wolverine shows erratic groups of four prints. It lives in remote areas and travels long distances.

COMMENTS Of the mustelids, only the Giant Otter and Sea Otter are larger than the Wolverine. It is a very strong animal with powerful jaws. It digs small rodents from their burrows and often hides food underground.

▼ *This Striped Skunk is poised to use its defensive weapon—a jet of foul-smelling fluid that it can shoot with great accuracy from its anal gland.*

Smelly Skunk

Skunks have an excellent way of defending themselves. If threatened by an attacker, a skunk first arches its back, lifts its tail high, and may even stand on its front feet. If all else fails, the skunk squirts out a vile-smelling liquid from special glands near its tail. The smell is so strong that it stops the victim from breathing for a short time. Meanwhile the skunk escapes, leaving behind a stench that can be smelled from as far as 1½ miles (2.5 km) away.

▲ A Kinkajou scrambles up a branch in search of fruit.
It can use its prehensile tail to grip branches while it climbs.

Raccoons and Coati

The raccoon family includes about 18 different species, including olingos, raccoons, and coati, as well as the Ringtail and the Kinkajou. They live in wooded areas of North and South America. All have a long body, thick tail, and short legs. They spend at least some of their time in trees. These mammals are carnivores but most also eat plants and fruit. Most raccoons are quite bold animals and are not difficult to spot in the wild.

Common Raccoon

SIZE Body: 22 in (55 cm); tail: 16 in (40 cm)
RANGE North, Central, and northern South America; introduced in Europe and Russia
HABITAT Woodland, usually near fresh water, towns, and cities
FOOD Frogs, crayfish, fish, nuts, seeds, berries
TRACKS AND SIGNS Tracks show five long toes on each foot and look rather like the print of a human hand. The hind print is around 3½ in (9 cm) long, the front slightly smaller. The heel often shows on the hind prints. Trails usually show tracks in pairs, one front foot next to the opposite back one.
COMMENTS These animals sometimes dunk their food in water, not to wash it but to wet the food, which helps them feel it better and decide what is good to eat.

Kinkajou

SIZE Body: 22 in (55 cm); tail: 22 in (55 cm)
RANGE Mexico to southern Brazil
HABITAT Forests
FOOD Mainly fruit, also flowers, leaves, insects, birds' eggs, small animals, honey
TRACKS AND SIGNS Kinkajous spend most of their time in trees, and it is very rare to find their tracks on the ground. When they do walk on the ground, their prints show five long toes and claws. The Kinkajou has flexible fingers rather like ours, which it uses to grip food. Listen for its chirping and barking calls.
COMMENTS Like some monkeys, the Kinkajou is an expert climber with a prehensile (gripping) tail. It uses the tail as an extra limb to help it hold on to branches.

▲ *This Common Raccoon has just rummaged through a garbage can for scraps, leaving its characteristic mess behind.*

South American Coati

SIZE Body: 26 in (65 cm); tail: 28 in (70 cm)
RANGE Tropical South America
HABITAT Forest and woodland
FOOD Fruit, small mammals, and other creatures such as spiders, centipedes, and insects
TRACKS AND SIGNS Also known as the Brown-nosed Coati, this animal has feet smaller than those of the raccoon, with shorter toes. Its hind tracks are about 1¾ in (4.5 cm) wide, and its prints usually show all five toes and claws. These animals are active during the day and are far from shy, so they are quite easy to spot. They climb trees to feed on fruit but spend most of their time on the ground.
COMMENTS Like raccoons, coati will look through garbage cans for food.

Ⓗ

Happy Eaters

One of the secrets of the Common Raccoon's success is its willingness to eat lots of different kinds of food. Animals that are not fussy are less likely to have trouble finding something to eat. The raccoon has very nimble fingers, able to pick leaves and berries as well as dig out juicy bits from shellfish. It is also skilled at finding its way into trash cans and outbuildings to feed on scraps and can even untie ropes and open jars.

A raccoon sorting through garbage is now a common nighttime sight in many towns and cities. Some people want to scare raccoons away from their backyard, but if you want to attract these animals in order to watch them, try putting out some of their favorite foods. These include peanuts, bread, and cat and dog food. Be careful not to put food out too regularly, though, or the animals will become dependent on your supplies. And make sure never to go too close or try to feed them by hand—they may bite!

Mongooses and Civets

Mongooses and civets are small carnivores. There are about 37 different types of mongoose, which all live in Africa and Asia. These ground-living animals have a long, slim body. Civets also have a long, slim body and tail, but most have catlike striped or spotted markings. Most civets are active at night and are good climbers.

▶ *A group of Meerkats is called a "mob" or a "gang." If a mob becomes too large, it may split into smaller mobs.*

White-tailed Mongoose

SIZE Body: 28 in (70 cm); tail: 19 in (48 cm)
RANGE Africa south of the Sahara (except the forests of west, southwest, or central Africa); southwest Arabia
HABITAT Savanna and grassland
FOOD Insects, snakes, other small animals, birds' eggs, fruit
TRACKS AND SIGNS The White-tailed Mongoose has five toes on each foot, but only four show in its tracks, which are about 1¾ in (4.5 cm) long. Strong claw marks can usually be seen, too, with the marks of the left and right claws appearing well behind the claw marks of the central toes.
COMMENTS This large mongoose does not live in big groups like the Meerkat does, and it generally moves alone or in pairs. It is usually active at night.

Meerkat or Suricate

SIZE Body: 14 in (35 cm); tail: 10 in (25 cm)
RANGE Southern Africa
HABITAT Dry open country
FOOD Insects and other small animals, eggs, plants
TRACKS AND SIGNS This mongoose has four toes on each foot, all of which show in its tracks, which measure about 1¼ in (3 cm) in length. Its claws, too, show clearly in the tracks. Those on the front feet are longer than those on the back. Look for holes around the tracks, which show where the animals have been digging for insects.

COMMENTS Meerkats live in large family groups of up to 30 animals, so you are likely to find lots of tracks in the same place. They are usually active during the day. Look for their underground burrows, which may have several different entrances.

African Civet

SIZE Body: 35 in (90 cm); tail: 18 in (45 cm)

RANGE Africa from south of the Sahara to northern and eastern South Africa

HABITAT Forest and savanna

FOOD Rodents and other small animals, reptiles, insects, fruit, plants; also eats carrion

TRACKS AND SIGNS Has five toes on its front and back feet but only four show in the tracks. Short claw marks also appear. Tracks are around 2¼ in (6 cm) long and look similar to those of a dog, but check for the small dip at the back edge of main pads. Look for droppings sites (latrines) near tracks. These may be used by several animals. Droppings will contain plant matter as well as hairs, feathers, and insect remains.

COMMENTS The African Civet secretes a smelly black fluid from a gland near its tail and uses it to mark rocks and trees in its home range.

Feeding Signs

Meerkats quite quickly get used to humans and can be wonderful to watch as they go about their daily routine. They live in very well-organized groups, which usually contain two or three families. These families share the duties of caring for the young and keeping guard. While most of the group feeds, one Meerkat acts as sentry, often sitting up on its hind legs for a better view. If it spots a predator, it barks loudly so the rest of the group can dive for cover or hide in their burrow. Other animals act as babysitters, keeping an eye on young while their parents are off searching for food.

▼ *These Meerkats are warming up in the early morning sun after a cold desert night. They absorb heat through their sparsely furred underside while standing on their hind legs.*

Burrows

Some mammals, including badgers and rabbits, are excellent diggers and make complex homes underground. Here, they give birth and keep their young warm and safe from predators. Moles, for example, spend nearly all their lives below ground and rarely come to the surface.

Badger Home

Badgers dig an underground burrow called a sett. It contains many passages and chambers, some for breeding and some for sleeping. Their sleeping chambers are lined with bedding material such as leaves, hay, and ferns. A badger sett is quite easy to spot as the entrance is much larger than that of a rabbit hole and usually wider than it is high. Look for bedding material outside—the badger often drops some and also sometimes puts bedding out to air during the day. You will also spot a spoil heap—a pile of soil and stones outside, that has been dug out by the badger. Look for well-trodden paths, too, and for signs of scratching on nearby trees.

▲ Badgers dig pits called latrines where they deposit their dung. The pits mark their territory.

▼ This well-established badger sett has several entrances and an underground latrine.

Spoil heap

Bedding put out to air

Entrance

Underground latrine pit

Nest chamber for cubs

Main sleeping chamber

Fox dens

Some fox dens, also called earths, are simple holes under a tree root or even beneath an old garden shed. Others have a number of entrances and exits and several tunnels. Look for trampled vegetation around the hole and food remains, such as bones and feathers. If you have found an entrance hole and you are not sure if it is a fox den, have a sniff. An inhabited den has a very strong smell.

▲ *At the entrance to their den, a pair of fox cubs play with a chick their mother has brought them to eat.*

Water vole

Water voles often dig burrows in riverbanks, creating several entrances above and below the water line. There may be a network of tunnels linked to a burrow that is lined with grass and rushes. Look for entrance holes, and you may also spot the water vole's lawn—an area of close-cropped grass where the vole has been feeding near the entrance to its den. In some parts of their range, water voles make their burrows some distance away from water in grassy meadows.

Moles and molehills

Moles make tunnels to move around in as well as for nesting. They dig runs near the surface, pushing up the earth as they go and leaving a little ridge along the ground. Nesting tunnels are much deeper, and the dug-out earth forms little piles on the surface known as molehills. Moles sometimes come out of their tunnels via molehills, but they always close up the exit holes after themselves.

▶ *Molehills like these are made from the earth moles have pushed up from their feeding tunnels deep underground.*

Rabbit Warren

A small entrance hole less than 8 in (20 cm) wide with piles of earth and little round droppings outside may belong to a rabbit family. Most American rabbit species use burrows abandoned by other animals, such as badgers. Only a few species, such as the European Rabbit, and the Pygmy Rabbit in America, dig their own burrows, or warrens, which contain living and nesting chambers lined with grass and rabbit fur.

▼ *This is a small section of a rabbit warren. Warrens may be many years old and have hundreds of entrances.*

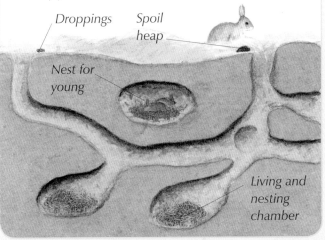

Droppings   Spoil heap

Nest for young

Living and nesting chamber

Bears

Bears are the largest meat-eating land mammals, but plants are a major part of the diet of Brown and Black Bears. Bears are big animals, with bulky bodies, big heads, and strong, short legs. They can be very dangerous, particularly if surprised, so they should be tracked only with an experienced person who knows what do to if you do have a close encounter.

▲ *The Brown Bear that left these scats in Kamchatka, eastern Russia, has been eating high-energy autumn berries to boost its fat reserves for the coming winter.*

◀ LIFE-SIZE *Brown Bear track*

Brown Bear (Grizzly Bear)

SIZE Body: 9¼ ft (2.8 m); tail: 8 in (20 cm)
RANGE Northern North America, northern Europe, parts of southern Europe, and Asia
HABITAT Mountains, tundra, forest, grassland
FOOD Mainly plant matter, including roots, bulbs, berries, nuts, grass; also eats insects, small mammals, fish
TRACKS AND SIGNS An animal as heavy as a Brown Bear leaves tracks on almost any surface. Hind footprints are up to 12 in (30 cm) long, showing the imprints of all five toes and the long claws. A walking bear leaves a trail of pairs of prints pointing slightly inward. Look out for piles of droppings, too, and for strands of hair caught on tree trunks.

COMMENTS Bears will scavenge on carrion, and if they find a large carcass may cover it to keep it safe from other animals. If you come across a partly hidden carcass, be very careful. A bear may be nearby and will want to protect its food.

◀ SCALE: ¹/₁₀ *life-size front track (top) and hind track (bottom)*

(H)

American Black Bear

SIZE Body: 6 ft (1.8 m); tail: 7 in (18 cm)
RANGE Canada, parts of United States, Mexico
HABITAT Wooded areas, mountains, national parks
FOOD Plant matter, including nuts, berries, grass, roots; also eats small mammals, fish, insects, carrion
TRACKS AND SIGNS The track of the hind foot looks a little like a human footprint but smaller and with claw marks. An important difference to look for is that the bear's big toe is on the outside of the foot— ours is on the inside. The tracks of the Black Bear's front foot are up to 6½ in (16 cm) long; hind foot tracks are up to 7 in (18 cm) long.
COMMENTS Black Bears live alone, except for mothers with cubs, but they do make some sounds, such as a loud rumbling growl or a breathy huffing sound. If you hear these, stay away.

◀ SCALE: ¹/₄ life-size

Polar Bear

SIZE Body: 11 ft (3.3 m); tail: 5 in (13 cm)
RANGE Arctic
HABITAT Coasts, ice floes
FOOD Seals are its main food, but it also eats sea birds, fish, and caribou; eats berries in summer
TRACKS AND SIGNS Thick fur on the Polar Bear's feet makes its tracks fuzzy. Its hind footprints are huge, at about 13 in (33 cm), and the tracks may not show all five claw marks.
COMMENTS A skilled and extremely powerful hunter that can move surprisingly fast and has an excellent sense of smell.

▲ SCALE: ¹/₇ life-size

▶ LIFE-SIZE
Polar Bear track

Telltale Signs

There are plenty of signs of the activity of Brown and Black Bears if you know what to look for. Black Bears are good climbers and will scramble up trees to reach fruit and nuts, leaving deep scratches on the bark (*see* Feeding Signs: Trees and Bushes, pages 60–61). Bears sometimes rip whole branches of fruit from trees, and you may also see logs that a bear has torn apart to get at insects inside. Brown Bears often dig for roots and small animals, and you may see the marks of their claws around the dug-up area.

Pandas

The Giant Panda and Red Panda are extraordinary animals and are seldom spotted in the wild. Scientists have long disagreed about which groups these two species belong to. At one time they were grouped together in their own family. Now most experts think that the Giant Panda belongs with the bears and the Red Panda with the raccoons. Destruction of their bamboo forest habitats is making both these animals rare.

◀ *A Giant Panda resting in the fork of a tree.*

Giant Panda

SIZE Body: 5 ft (1.5 m); tail: 4 in (10 cm)
RANGE Parts of central China
HABITAT Bamboo forest
FOOD Bamboo shoots, leaves, and stems; sometimes eats other plants, such as grasses and crocuses, as well as fish and small mammals
TRACKS AND SIGNS Giant Pandas are extremely difficult to track in the wild. Very shy, they can smell humans from a long way off and take care to stay well away. They even stay away from each other! You might see footprints of up to 7 in (18 cm) in length or perhaps other signs, such as chewed bamboo or evidence of a nest in a hollow tree or cave.
COMMENTS Pandas mark their range to help avoid straying into each other's territory. They spray urine onto bushes and tree trunks, claw bark, and also leave scent marks using special secretions from glands near the tail. To do this, a Giant Panda may back up against a tree or even stand on its front paws to rub its backside against the bark.

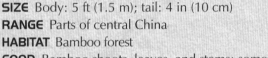

Red Panda

SIZE Body: 26 in (65 cm); tail: 19 in (48 cm)

RANGE Himalayas, Burma, northeast India, western China

HABITAT Mountain bamboo forests

FOOD Bamboo, grasses, fruits, roots, insects, eggs, birds

TRACKS AND SIGNS Red Pandas, like Giant Pandas, are very difficult to spot in the wild. They do move on the ground but spend much of their time up in the trees, where they are perfectly camouflaged among the reddish moss that covers the branches. Their tracks are small and neat, showing five toes and claws. Red Pandas mark their territories with droppings, urine, and secretions from glands near the tail.

COMMENTS The Red Panda is mostly active at night. It sometimes moves around in small family groups. Its young stay with their mother for at least a year.

Bamboo Eater

The Giant Panda's main food is bamboo, and it eats as many as 30 different kinds. There is not much nutrition in bamboo, so the panda spends as many as 12 hours a day feeding in order to get what it needs. One animal may eat up to 28 lb (12.5 kg) of bamboo every day. The panda's hands are specially designed for holding bamboo stems. It has an extra thumb-like digit, which is actually part of the wrist bone. The panda can hold this digit against its first finger, allowing it to pick and hold bamboo stems. Its large flat teeth are well-suited to its tough diet, and it also has very strong jaw muscles to cope with the work of chewing.

▲ The Red Panda's curved, sharp claws help it seize fruit and leaves and keep a strong grip while climbing along narrow tree branches.

Hyenas

Hyenas may look like dogs, but they are a separate group of meat-eating mammals. The front of the body is more heavily built than the back, and the body slopes down toward the tail. They often scavenge on the kills of other hunters, but they are also predators themselves. The Spotted Hyena is an efficient killer and has jaws so strong it can crunch bones. The Aardwolf belongs to the same family but has a smaller head and teeth and feeds almost entirely on termites. Hyenas are dangerous and should be tracked only with an experienced guide.

▲ *The hunter becomes the defender as a pack of Spotted Hyenas closes in on a lioness after she has made her kill.*

Aardwolf

SIZE Body: 26 in (67 cm); tail: 10 in (25 cm)
RANGE Eastern and southern Africa
HABITAT Open plains and bush
FOOD Insects, mainly termites
TRACKS AND SIGNS Footprints are about 2¼ in (6 cm) long. The Aardwolf has five toes on its front foot, but only four show on tracks as the fifth is too high. There are four toes on the hind foot and claws show on both prints. Look for oval-shaped piles of droppings, partly covered with earth.
COMMENTS The Aardwolf has very good hearing and can hear termites coming up to the ground surface at night. It then laps them up by the thousand with its long, sticky tongue.

Spotted Hyena

SIZE Body: 4½ ft (1.4 m); tail: 12 in (30 cm)
RANGE Much of sub-Saharan Africa
HABITAT Savanna and semi-desert
FOOD When hunting in packs, Spotted Hyenas can bring down large prey such as wildebeest and zebra; they also hunt a wide range of other prey, including antelope, the young of hippos and giraffes, and smaller mammals such as hares.
TRACKS AND SIGNS Tracks show four toes and claws. Front and hind prints are both up to 4¼ in (11 cm) long. Look for piles of droppings placed at territory boundaries.
COMMENTS Listen for the so-called "laughing" sound the hyena makes when attacked or chased.

▲ *A ravenous pack of Spotted Hyenas devours the juicy bones of an antelope in Kenya. They can strip the flesh in minutes, crunch the bones to powdery chips, and chew through the toughest gristle and skin, leaving only the horns and teeth.*

Latrine Sites

Spotted and Brown Hyenas leave their droppings in special areas of their territory called latrines. The droppings of Spotted Hyenas are white in color due to the large amount of bone the animals eat. A Spotted Hyena latrine may cover a wide area, and the droppings may be very scattered. The droppings of the Brown Hyena are smaller than those of its spotted cousin and brownish in color, because the animal eats less bone and more fruit than its relative. A Brown Hyena latrine is usually in a slight dip in the ground.

Brown Hyena

SIZE Body: 4¼ ft (1.3 m); tail: 10 in (25 cm)

RANGE Southern Africa

HABITAT Open scrub, savanna, semi-desert

FOOD Scavenges the remains of large prey killed by other hunters; also eats rats, mice, insects, birds' eggs, fruit

TRACKS AND SIGNS Trail shows footprints with four toes and claws on each foot. The front footprint is up to 4 in (10.5 cm) long, 1 in (2.5 cm) longer than the hind footprint, an important difference from the track of the Spotted Hyena.

COMMENTS The Brown Hyena sometimes stores food under bushes or in holes and comes back to find it a day or so later.

Chimpanzees and Gorillas

The great apes belong to the mammal group called primates—which also includes us. Apes live in groups and are very intelligent. They have hands similar to ours. Chimpanzees use tools such as stones to get food. Apes usually walk on all fours, leaning on the knuckles of their hands. All the great apes are very rare. They should be tracked only in the company of guides who understand their behavior.

▲ Like gorillas, chimpanzees walk on all fours, with their hands curled so that only the knuckles leave marks.

Bonobo

◄ SCALE: ¹/₅ life-size

SIZE Body: 32½ in (83 cm); tail: none
RANGE Central Africa
HABITAT Rain forest
FOOD Mainly fruit, but also leaves, seeds, and small creatures such as worms
TRACKS AND SIGNS Bonobos are a type of chimpanzee. Their tracks are very like those of the Common Chimpanzee but the two species don't live in the same areas. The feet are around 7½ in (19 cm) long. Bonobos make loud calls to warn other members of the group of danger or to alert them to a food source.
COMMENTS Look out for Bonobo nests. Like Common Chimps, they make nests in trees to sleep in at night by weaving branches together. They may line their nests with leaves.

Ⓗ

▶ LIFE-SIZE hind track of Common Chimpanzee

Common Chimpanzee

SIZE Body: 36 in (92 cm); tail: none
RANGE Western and central Africa: Guinea and Sierra Leone to Uganda and Tanzania
HABITAT Tropical rain forests, including mountain forests, and savanna
FOOD Plants, including leaves, fruit, and seeds, but also insects, eggs, occasionally prey such as baboons and monkeys
TRACKS AND SIGNS Footprint is wider than that of the Bonobo and about 7½ in (19 cm) long. Look for droppings that contain mostly plant remains.
COMMENTS Chimps use sticks to extract insects such as termites from their nests and to hook down fruit from branches. They also use stones to crack nuts and leaves as sponges to soak up water.

▶ SCALE: ¹/₅ life-size

Ⓗ

Western Gorilla

(H)   ◄ SCALE: ¹/₇ *life-size*

SIZE Body: 6¼ ft (1.9 m); tail: none

RANGE Central and East Africa

HABITAT Tropical rain forests of Central Africa; (Mountain Gorillas live in cloud forests on the Virunga Volcanoes, East Africa)

FOOD Mainly leaves, shoots, stems, and some fruits, flowers, and insects

TRACKS AND SIGNS The footprint is up to about 11 in (28 cm) long, and the big toe stands away from the side of the foot like a thumb. Only the knuckles of the hands show in the front tracks. Gorillas make many loud calls to keep in touch with others in the troop, so you may hear them even if you cannot see them.

COMMENTS Gorillas are active during the day and sleep in tree nests at night, which they make fresh every day. They usually move only a mile or two a day as they feed.

▲ *Chimpanzee scats often contain fruit seeds, which become scattered around the forest to grow into new plants.*

Handprints

The prints shown for the primates on these pages are all hind tracks. Gorillas and chimpanzees do not make full handprints, only little rounded marks made as they lean on their knuckles. Try making your own knuckle prints on a soft surface such as damp sand to see what these look like.

Gibbons and Orangutans

Orangutans are great apes, like chimpanzees and gorillas. They are tree dwellers and rarely walk on the ground. Gibbons, also called the lesser apes, are well adapted for life in the trees, climbing and swinging from branch to branch very skillfully. Gibbons and orangutans live in Asia, and their tracks are very rare.

▶ *A gibbon's wrists have flexible ball-and-socket joints, which help it to swing smoothly from branch to branch.*

Orangutan

SIZE Body: 5 ft (1.5 m); tail: none
RANGE Borneo and Sumatra
HABITAT Tropical rain forest
FOOD Mainly fruit; also leaves, insects, perhaps small animals and birds' eggs
TRACKS AND SIGNS There are two species of orangutan, the Bornean and Sumatran. Both are extremely rare, so you would be very lucky to see one. But just in case, look very carefully at trees that are fruiting, particularly those such as durian, which orangutans love. Check for signs of tree nests made by the apes, large branches moving, and piles of fruit skins under trees. And listen for the males' loud roaring call.
COMMENTS Like chimpanzees, the orangutan has been spotted using tools in the wild. It drapes large leaves over itself for shelter from the sun or rain and uses sticks to scratch itself or to extract insects from nests. It also uses sticks to help it reach fruit at the end of branches.

Black Gibbon

SIZE Body: 26 in (65 cm); tail: none
RANGE Southeastern China, parts of Laos and Vietnam
HABITAT Tropical rain forest
FOOD Mainly fruit; also eats leaves, insects, and other small creatures
TRACKS AND SIGNS You are much more likely to hear gibbons than see them, as most of their activity takes place in the treetops high above your head. But they do make a wide range of loud calls to keep in touch with each other, warn of danger, and defend their territory. Some of these calls can be heard several miles away. Males and females may sing "duets" together.
COMMENTS Gibbons don't make nests but just sleep while sitting up in the trees.

Swinging Gibbons

Gibbons are the most acrobatic of all tree-living animals and travel through the trees at amazing speed. They swing from branch to branch on their long arms in a form of movement called brachiation. A gibbon rarely uses its feet for grasping but often swings its legs forward to help propel it to the next handhold. Sometimes the gibbon will even let go both hands and just leap through the air to the next tree.

▼ *Like gorillas, orangutans make a new nest from branches and leaves each evening. This Sumatran Orangutan has made her nest in a tree and is sitting in it with her young.*

Hoolock Gibbon

SIZE Body: 26 in (65 cm); tail: none
RANGE India, Bangladesh, Burma
HABITAT Tropical rain forest
FOOD Mainly fruit; also eats leaves, insects, and other small creatures
TRACKS AND SIGNS Tracks are almost never seen, as this animal rarely comes down to the ground. Listen for this gibbon's very loud screeching calls.
COMMENTS Gibbons live in family groups of a male, a female, and their young.

▲ *Groups, or troops, of baboons, such as these Olive Baboons in Tanzania, usually stay close to lakes or rivers.*

Old World Monkeys

Monkeys live in family groups and are agile and sociable. They can be difficult to track, as they are usually way above our heads, but you can look out for tracks, signs of feeding, such as fruit skins, and droppings. Monkeys are noisy, and you are more likely to hear them than see them. The monkeys of the "Old World"—those in Africa and Asia—differ from monkeys in Central and South America, part of the "New World."

Chacma Baboon

◀ SCALE: ¼ *life-size*

Ⓗ

SIZE Body: 30 in (75 cm); tail: 25 in (65 cm)
RANGE Southern Africa
HABITAT Savanna, open woodland, and scrub
FOOD Plant foods, such as grass, leaves, flowers, and fruits; also eats insects and even small mammals
TRACKS AND SIGNS This monkey moves around in large groups of 100 or more animals. Usually active during the day. Tracks show footprints that are 6 in (15 cm) long—twice as long as the hands. Only the front part of the hand and the thumb appears in tracks. You may also hear a barking call as members of the troop shout to one another.
COMMENTS Signs that baboons have been feeding include stems ripped off plants and only parts of the plants eaten.

◀ LIFE-SIZE *footprint of Chacma Baboon*

Vervet Monkey

SIZE Body: 24 in (60 cm); tail: 28 in (70 cm)
RANGE Southern Africa
HABITAT Savanna, rain forest edge, woodland
FOOD Leaves, fruit, flowers, and insects
TRACKS AND SIGNS The Vervet spends more time on the ground than many other monkeys, so its tracks are more likely to be seen. Prints are 3¼–4 in (8–10 cm) long. You may also see imprints of the long tails where they have sat down to feed. Monkey oranges are a favorite food, and the skins may be left on the ground.
COMMENTS Vervets live in troops of 20 or more animals. They search for food on the ground and in trees but always sleep up in trees at night.

Ⓗ

SCALE: ½ *life-size* ▶

◀ LIFE-SIZE *footprint of Vervet Monkey*

▲ *Baboons like to sit on prominent rocks and watch for danger, and they often leave scats behind. These Gelada Baboon scats show that the animal has been eating a favorite food—grass.*

▲ *This Olive Baboon scat, found on a riverbank in Kenya, shows the remains of crayfish, a popular food with several baboon species.*

Hand Shapes

Most monkeys have hands similar to those of humans, which they can use to pick up small items of food, such as leaves and fruit. Except for colobus monkeys, they have thumbs, which they can move independently of their fingers and place against one of the fingers in order to hold things.

Monkey
Long fingers for gripping branches, short thumb.

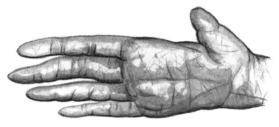

Baboon
Longer thumb for gripping and holding small objects.

Human
Long thumb enables precision grip.

Black-and-white Colobus

SIZE Body: 26 in (65 cm); tail: 3 ft (90 cm)
RANGE Central Africa
HABITAT Rain forest on lowlands and mountains, including bamboo forest
FOOD Mainly leaves; also eats some unripe fruit
TRACKS AND SIGNS Colobus monkeys spend a lot of time in the trees feeding on leaves, and are not often seen on the ground. If you do find colobus tracks, they will show long, thin fingers and toes with no thumbmarks on the handprints, as this monkey has no thumbs. Its footprints, which do show thumbs, are about 4 in (10 cm) long. Droppings contain leaf fiber, so they look different from the droppings of fruit-eating monkeys.
COMMENTS This monkey lives in groups of 25 or so and is most active in the morning and early evening. It sleeps in trees at night to avoid predators. The male group leader makes a loud roaring call to warn others off his territory.

▶ SCALE: ¹/₂ life-size

Ⓗ

◀ LIFE-SIZE *footprint of Black-and-white Colobus*

▲ *A Black Spider Monkey uses its tail to help it dangle from a branch while searching for fruit.*

New World Monkeys

There are more than 40 different kinds of New World monkeys living in the forests of Central and South America. Many New World monkeys have a prehensile, or gripping, tail, which they can use like a fifth limb when climbing and moving from tree to tree. These expert tree climbers are rarely seen on the ground, so they are difficult to track, but you may hear their loud calls as they shout to one another.

Red Howler

SIZE Body: 28 in (70 cm); tail: 30 in (75 cm)
RANGE Northern South America
HABITAT Tropical rain forest, mangrove swamps
FOOD Leaves, fruit, and other plant matter
TRACKS AND SIGNS Howlers spend most of their time in the treetops; at night they sleep on branches. If you are in their territory but do not see them, you will hear these monkeys. Males in a troop all roar together, especially in early morning and late afternoon, a deafening howl answered by males in other troops and heard 3 miles (5 km) away.
COMMENTS The Red Howler is one of the largest of the New World monkeys. It lives in groups of up to 12 animals and is usually active in the daytime.

Common Woolly Monkey

SIZE Body: 24 in (60 cm); tail: 32 in (80 cm)
RANGE South America: Amazon basin
HABITAT Tropical rain forest
FOOD Fruit, leaves, and some insects
TRACKS AND SIGNS Woolly monkeys do sometimes come down to the ground, but they are mainly tree dwellers, swinging from branch to branch on their long tails. When on the ground, they walk upright using their arms to help them balance. Watch for males shaking branches to warn off rival males and listen for loud barking calls or screams that alert the rest of the troop to any possible danger.
COMMENTS Woolly monkeys live in large groups of 30 or more animals.

▲ *Like all howlers, this Mantled Howler has an incredibly loud voice. The volume is due to its specially adapted voice box, or larynx, which is much larger than in most animals and acts as an echo chamber for the monkey's howls. Males shout to defend their territories—the bigger the territory, the louder their call.*

Black Spider Monkey

SIZE Body: 24 in (60 cm);
tail: 32 in (80 cm)
RANGE Northern South America
HABITAT Tropical rain forest
FOOD Fruit, nuts, seeds, leaves, insects, and eggs
TRACKS AND SIGNS Like howler monkeys, spider monkeys rarely come to the ground, but you may catch a glimpse of them swinging in the treetops. Listen for their loud barks and screams.
COMMENTS The Black Spider Monkey is almost as agile as the gibbons and is the most acrobatic of all the New World monkeys. It looks as though it has five legs, as it uses its prehensile (gripping) tail as an extra limb.

An Extra Limb

Most monkeys have long tails, which help them balance as they climb and leap in the treetops. South American monkeys, such as the howlers and spider monkeys, have a special tail that also acts as an extra limb. This is called a prehensile, or gripping, tail. It has strong muscles that can curl round branches and support the monkey's entire weight as it swings from branch to branch and stops to feed. The underside of the tail has no fur and is crisscrossed with grooves to help increase grip.

Bats

Bats are the only mammals that truly fly, powering themselves through the air on their large wings. Most bats are active during the night and spend the day asleep, hanging upside down from branches or ledges in caves. Some bats feed on fruit, but most catch insects to eat. Many find their food by means of echolocation. They make high-pitched sounds that bounce, or echo, off nearby objects. The bats use these echoes to locate their prey and avoid obstacles. In some areas bats may carry the disease rabies, so never go near one if you see it on the ground.

▲ Like most bat droppings, these from Greater Mouse-eared Bats in Spain are dark and crumbly to the touch. They contain indigestible insect parts, such as wings and legs.

Greater Fruit Bat

SIZE Body: 16 in (40 cm); wingspan: 5 ft (1.5 m); tail: none
RANGE South and Southeast Asia
HABITAT Forest
FOOD Fruit—the bat crushes the fruit with its peglike teeth to get the juice and spits out the seeds and flesh
TRACKS AND SIGNS You may see the remains of fruit under feeding trees.
COMMENTS Fruit bats are also known as flying-fox bats. This one is sometimes called the Indian Flying Fox and has one of the biggest wingspans of any bat. During the day it roosts in trees in flocks of several thousand animals.

Greater Horseshoe Bat

SIZE Body: 5 (12.5 cm); wingspan: 14 in (35 cm); tail: 1½ in (4 cm)
RANGE Europe, Asia, North Africa
HABITAT Forested areas, open country, and caves
FOOD Insects, such as beetles, moths, and flies
TRACKS AND SIGNS These bats swoop down to the ground to catch insects, particularly beetles, but their tracks are rarely found. Look for their droppings, which are dark brown or black and contain insect remains, such as wings and wing cases.
COMMENTS A large pile of insect-filled droppings beneath a tree or a loft is a sure sign that a colony of bats is roosting above.

In the Air

Bats can fly just as well as birds. Their wings are made of thin skin and supported by the bones of the arms and hands. The "finger" bones are extra long, and these are the main supports of the wings. A bat's wings extend down the sides of the body and legs.

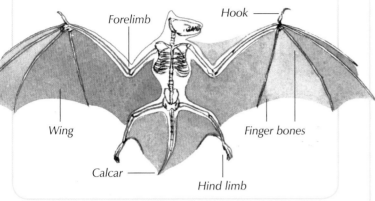

Forelimb · Hook · Wing · Finger bones · Calcar · Hind limb

American False Vampire

SIZE Body: 5 in (13 cm); wingspan: 3¼ ft (1 m); tail: none
RANGE Mexico, Central and South America
HABITAT Forests
FOOD Birds, rodents, other bats; may eat some fruit and insects
TRACKS AND SIGNS This bat sometimes stalks mice on the ground as well as hunting birds in trees.
COMMENTS This is the largest bat in North or South America. It is called "false vampire" because people used to think it fed on blood like the vampire bat.

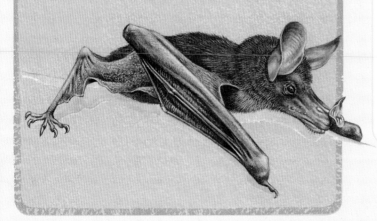

On Land

Bats are experts in the air but can only crawl along on land with the help of their back feet and the claws on each first finger. Trails are rarely seen, but if you do find bat tracks, the hind prints will usually show all five toes and claws, while the front prints will show only the claw mark of the first finger on each front limb. Usually a bat walks or runs like other mammals, moving its legs in diagonally opposite pairs, but sometimes bats "leapfrog" along the ground, moving both front legs as a pair and then both back legs.

Running on land	Leapfrogging on land

Feeding Signs TREES AND BUSHES

Lots of mammals feed on the leaves and buds of trees, and even on bark and twigs. The signs of their feeding activity are everywhere if you know where to look. Check for chewed and bitten twigs, scratched and stripped bark, and tooth marks on bark and branches. Think about how big the animal might have been. Are the marks of its activity high up or near the ground? Are tooth marks large or small?

▼ *This tree's bark has been stripped by a bison rubbing against it. The animal has left some of its fur behind.*

Beavers

Beavers probably leave more feeding signs than any other animal, as they feed on bark, twigs, and leaves, and also cut down trees to use in building their lodges and dams.

Favorite feeding trees include aspen, alder, willow, and birch. To cut down a tree, a beaver gnaws all around the trunk until it topples over. Large tooth marks can be seen on the trunk.

Smaller plant eaters

Small tooth marks and chewed bark near ground level are usually the work of voles. They feed on bark in winter and strip new shoots in spring and summer, often damaging young trees. Rabbits and hares, too, feed from the base of trees, removing bark and leaving the marks of their large incisor teeth. Squirrels feed higher up and may take off long strips of bark as well as eating nuts and buds.

◄ *These trees have been felled by beavers. The beavers carry the branches away to use as building material for their dam or lodge. They also feed on the bark.*

Bears

If you see deep claw marks on trees and signs of peeled bark, a Black Bear has probably been in action. Bears often strip off the outer layer of bark to feed on the softer inner layer. They also leave claw marks as they climb to reach fruit and berries or tear off whole branches as they feed. Black Bears and Grizzly Bears also scratch tree trunks as a sign that this is their territory, warning other bears to keep away.

▼ *Black Bears often leave scratch marks when climbing trees.*

▲ *The bark on this tree has been peeled away by an animal, probably a Black Bear.*

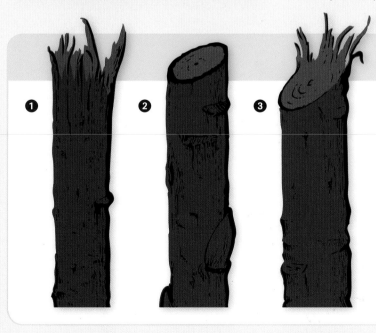

❶ ❷ ❸

Who Did This?

Rabbits and hares have big front teeth. To feed, they bite through twigs and shoots, leaving a clean edge. Grazers, such as Elk and Moose, do not have sharp front teeth. They twist off twigs, leaving a ragged edge behind. Which animals do you think have been feeding on these bushes?

❶ Moose ❷ Hare ❸ Elk

Elephants

Elephants are the world's largest land animals, some weighing more than 16,500 lb (7,500 kg). There are two species of elephant. One lives in Africa and the other in India and Southeast Asia. Both species have a trunk—a long nose fixed to the upper lip—which they use for smelling, feeding, drinking, breathing, and for making loud trumpeting calls. Elephant females and young live in family groups of up to 20 animals. Male elephants usually gather in separate herds.

▲ *These small birds in Namibia, Africa, are searching in fresh elephant dung for nutritious seeds.*

Asian Elephant

SIZE Body, including trunk: 21 ft (6.4 m); tail 4 ft (1.2 m)
RANGE India and Southeast Asia
HABITAT Forests and grasslands
FOOD A wide range of plant food, including leaves, grass, fruit, bark, twigs
TRACKS AND SIGNS Tracks are similar to those of the African Elephant, but slightly smaller, with five toes on each front foot and four on each hind foot. They leave plenty of evidence of their feeding activities, as well as scratches on trees where they rub themselves against the bark to soothe an itch or rid themselves of parasites.
COMMENTS Elephants may seem to be destructive but in fact their activities are very important for other wildlife. They make pathways that are used by other animals; they dig water holes that can be used by many creatures; and by clearing vegetation, they make room for new plants to grow, and also spread seeds from fruits and vegetables over a wide area.

◀ SCALE: ¹/₁₀ *life-size front footprint*

Ⓗ

◀ SCALE: ¹/₁₀ *life-size hind footprint*

LIFE-SIZE *footprint of African Elephant* ▶

African Elephant

SIZE Body, including trunk: 24½ ft (7.5 m); tail 5 ft (1.5 m)
RANGE Africa south of the Sahara; once more widespread
HABITAT Varied, including forests, swamps, grassland
FOOD Leaves, grass, bark, twigs, roots, fruit, and other plant material
TRACKS AND SIGNS Elephant tracks are so huge that you can't mistake them. The African Elephant has three or four toes on each hind foot and four or five on each front foot, but these are covered with a thick pad made of springy elastic material. The large hooflike "toenails" are horny pads on the skin. The front track is circular and up to 20 in (50 cm) long and shows the ridges on the surface of the footpads. Each elephant leaves individual ridge patterns, which helps trackers identify the trails of individuals. Hind foot tracks are slightly longer than the front tracks and more oval in shape.

COMMENTS Because they are so large, elephants leave many signs of their presence and feeding activities. They crush vegetation as they walk, pull up trees by the roots to feed, and break off branches. They also pull off strips of tree bark to eat. Elephants may eat as much as 440 lb (200 kg) of plant food in a day.

Ⓗ

▲ SCALE: ¹/₁₀ life-size front footprint

▶ SCALE: ¹/₁₀ life-size hind footprint

What's the Difference?

The two elephant species are very similar but the African Elephant is larger and heavier than the Asian. It has larger ears and its back also dips slightly in the middle, while the Asian Elephant's has a rounded, slightly humped shape. The African Elephant's trunk has two fingerlike projections at the end, while the Asian Elephant has only one. In African Elephants both sexes have tusks, but in Asian Elephants usually only the males do.

Trunk tip of African

Trunk tip of Asian

Zebras and Giraffes

Zebras and horses belong to a family of eight fast-running mammal species with a single hoof on each foot that has developed from the third toe. Wild horses and zebras live in herds and feed mostly on grass. Wild horses are officially extinct in the wild, although some horses bred in captivity have been released into the wild. The Giraffe belongs to a separate family, which contains only one other species, the Okapi. Both species have cloven hooves.

◄ *A herd of zebras drinks at a water hole. Like horses, they have teeth adapted for cropping and chewing grass.*

Burchell's Zebra

SIZE Body: 8 ft (2.4 m); tail: 22 in (55 cm)

RANGE Africa: Angola to South Africa

HABITAT Grassland, woodland

FOOD Mostly grass but also browses on bushes

TRACKS AND SIGNS The front hoof track is rounder and slightly larger than the hind track, at about 4 in (10 cm) long. Look for piles of kidney-shaped droppings.

COMMENTS The different species of zebra are similar, but this zebra has yellow stripes between the black stripes along its sides.

Mustang

SIZE
Body length: 9¼ ft (2.8 m); tail: 24 in (60 cm)

RANGE Western North America

HABITAT Grassland

FOOD Grass and leaves

TRACKS AND SIGNS Like all horses, the mustang has a single toe on each foot and leaves a large, almost circular track. The track is clearly different from the horseshoe print left by a shoed domestic horse. Look for signs of the horses browsing on leaves and for their dung. Mustangs generally travel in herds.

COMMENTS Mustangs live wild, but they are descended from domesticated horses. The original mustangs were from Spanish horses but today they are a mixture of breeds.

Giraffe

SIZE Body: up to 19 ft (5.8 m); tail: 3¼ ft (1 m)
RANGE Africa south of the Sahara; once more widespread
HABITAT Dry savanna, open woodland
FOOD Browses on the leaves of acacia and other trees
TRACKS AND SIGNS Tracks are easy to recognize. They are longer than those of other cloven-hoofed animals, at 8–10 in (20–25 cm) long. Droppings are larger than those of antelope and usually scattered as they fall from quite a height.
COMMENTS The world's tallest animal, the Giraffe is unmistakable. Males can be up to 19 ft (5.8 m) tall.

◀ SCALE: ¹/₅ *life-size*

Horse Hooves

A horse, like a zebra, has only one toe on each foot. It walks on the tips of these toes, which are covered with a hard hoof made of bone. Underneath the hoof is a thick rubbery pad, which helps protect the horse and absorbs impact as it walks. The size of the hoof varies greatly according to the type of horse, but it makes a rounded track with a notch in the hind edge. Domestic horses are often fitted with metal horseshoes that fit around the outside rim of the hoof for extra protection. In shod horses, only the outline of the shoe shows in tracks.

Horse's hoof without shoe

Horse's hoof with shoe

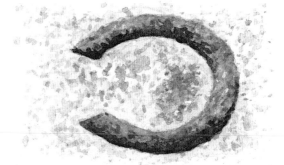

◀ LIFE-SIZE *footprint of Giraffe*

Rhinos and Tapirs

▲ *This male White Rhino in Kenya is marking its territory by kicking its dung vigorously to spread it around.*

There are five living species of rhinoceros, and all are now rare. Rhinos are large animals with thick skin that falls into folds. They have one or two horns on the head, which males use in fights with rivals. Tapirs are much smaller and have a piglike body. Rhinoceroses and tapirs are odd-toed, hoofed animals. Rhinos have three toes on each foot, while tapirs have three toes on their hind feet, but an extra toe on each front foot. Rhinos do not see well and are likely to charge if they hear anything unfamiliar.

White Rhinoceros

◄ SCALE: ¹/₁₀ *life-size*

SIZE Body: 14 ft (4.3 m); tail: 28 in (70 cm)
RANGE Scattered areas of northeastern and southern Africa, generally now only in protected reserves
HABITAT Savanna
FOOD Grass and other plants
TRACKS AND SIGNS The tracks of this huge animal show its three large toes, each of which has a wide, thick nail. Its footprints are about 12 in (30 cm) long. The prints of the Black Rhino are similar but slightly smaller, with a smaller indent in the back edge.
COMMENTS Check rhino droppings to see whether you're following a White or a Black Rhino. White Rhinos eat mostly grass, so their droppings contain fine material. Black Rhinos, in contrast, browse on bushes and trees, so their droppings contain coarser, woody fragments.

Indian Rhinoceros

◀ SCALE: ¹/₁₀ life-size

SIZE Body: 12½ ft (3.8 m); tail: 32 in (80 cm)
RANGE Small area of northeastern India; once more widespread
HABITAT Grassland, floodplains, wooded meadows
FOOD Grass, aquatic plants, other plants
TRACKS AND SIGNS Tracks are similar to those of the White Rhino but with no indent at the back edge. Signs that rhinos are close by include large piles of droppings, called middens, near mud wallows and paths. There may be horn marks gouged into the ground around the piles. Male rhinos also spray urine to mark their territory.
COMMENTS Rhinos love to wallow in muddy water to cool themselves down and escape biting flies. Look for hollows in the mud made by the rhino's huge body. There may also be marks where the animal has rubbed its muddy body against a tree.

Brazilian Tapir

◀ SCALE: ¹/₁₀ life-size

SIZE Body: 6½ ft (2 m); tail: 3¼ ft (1 m)
RANGE South America: Venezuela to Argentina
HABITAT Rain forest and woodland, always near water
FOOD Aquatic plants, fruit, stems of land plants
TRACKS AND SIGNS Look for the paths worn down by tapirs on their way to water, as they quickly flatten any vegetation. This animal is often on muddy ground, so its distinctive three-toed tracks, which are up to 7 in (18 cm) long, are frequently seen, but the creature itself is more difficult to spot.
COMMENTS Tapirs are good swimmers. If they become frightened, they will plunge into water to escape if they can.

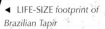
◀ LIFE-SIZE *footprint of Brazilian Tapir*

Hippos

There are only two kinds of hippopotamus, both of which live in Africa. The full-sized Hippo moves easily in water and can even walk along the river bottom. Its nostrils close off so it does not get water in its nose. It spends its days resting in the water and comes out at night to feed on land. The Pygmy Hippo also feeds at night. Hippos have almost hairless skin, which dries out if not regularly submerged. Although they are plant eaters, they can be very dangerous. Track a hippo only with an experienced guide.

◄ LIFE-SIZE
Hippo track

Pygmy Hippopotamus

SIZE
Body: 6 ft (1.8 m);
tail: 8 in (20 cm)
RANGE West Africa
HABITAT Tropical rain forest and swamps
FOOD Water plants, leaves, grass, fallen fruit
TRACKS AND SIGNS Tracks are similar to those of its larger relative but about half the size and narrower. The toes are also more splayed out and only the front feet have webbing. This hippo spends more time on land, so its trail is seen more often.
COMMENTS The Pygmy Hippo usually lives alone, except for females with young. It is very rare and has long been hunted for its meat.

◄ A dominant male marks his territory by wagging his tail to scatter his dung around. The scattered dung acts as a warning to other males that they should act submissively or expect a fight. Groups of female Hippos live with their young in the territory of a dominant male.

Yawning Hippos

A Hippo can open its huge mouth amazingly wide, revealing large teeth protruding as much as 12 in (30 cm) above the gum. But if you do see a Hippo yawn, beware. It isn't tired—this is actually a threat display, and Hippos have been known to charge when disturbed.

Hippopotamus

SIZE Body: 14 ft (4.3 m); tail: 22 in (56 cm)
RANGE Parts of eastern and southern Africa south of the Sahara
HABITAT Rivers and lakes in grassland
FOOD Grass
TRACKS AND SIGNS The Hippo has large feet, 10 in (26 cm) long, to support its great bulk, so its tracks are usually very clear and cannot be mistaken for those of any other animal. It has four toes on each foot, with heavy, hooflike nails. The front feet are slightly larger than the hind feet, and there is webbing between the toes on all four feet. The droppings are barrel-shaped and smaller than those of the other African giants—the African Elephant and two rhino species. Male Hippos may scatter their droppings on bushes to mark their territory. They tend to use the same routes when feeding, so look for well-worn paths of flattened grass.
COMMENTS The Hippo spends much of its time in water, with its huge body mostly submerged. Often just its eyes, ears, and nose can be seen above the surface. It usually lives in groups of 15 or more animals.

◄ SCALE: ⅓ life-size

▲ *These dry, hard nuggets are typical of Moose scat in the winter, when the animal eats mainly twigs and bark.*

Deer

The 40 or so species of deer are all even-toed, long-legged plant eaters. The males of most species grow big bony antlers on their heads each year, which fall off after the mating season. You may find these in winter, unless the deer have eaten them to obtain calcium. Deer have four toes and walk on the middle two, which form the two sides (cleaves) of their cloven (split) hooves. The smaller outer toes, or dewclaws, behind and above the hoof do not always show in tracks. Larger deer, such as Moose, Elk, and Caribou, usually leave clear tracks.

Moose

SIZE Body: up to 10½ ft (3.2 m); tail: 4 in (10 cm)
RANGE Northern North America, Europe, Asia
HABITAT Forest, often near water
FOOD Water plants; leaves, twigs, and bark from trees and bushes
TRACKS AND SIGNS The cloven (split) fore hooves leave tracks about 4 in (10 cm) wide and pointed at the tips. In softer ground, dewclaws may show. Moose tracks are easy to confuse with domestic cattle tracks, but are more pointed and more likely to show dewclaws. You may also spot wide paths through forested areas where Moose live.
COMMENTS The Moose is shy, despite being the world's largest deer, and usually avoids humans. The male's huge antlers are up to 6½ ft (2 m) wide, with a broad, flattened shape and many branches.

▶ SCALE: ⅓ life-size

Elk or Wapiti

SIZE Body: 8½ ft (2.6 m); tail: 10½ in (27 cm)
RANGE Europe, Asia, northwestern and parts of eastern North America to Mexico; introduced in New Zealand, Australia
HABITAT Forest and grassland, but very adaptable
FOOD Grass and woody plants
TRACKS AND SIGNS Elk tracks show fairly broad cloven hooves about 2–3 in (5–7.5 cm) wide; the dewclaws are not usually visible. The two parts of the print are fairly parallel compared with those of other deer.
COMMENTS Male Elk have large, slender, branching antlers, and in winter they may have a mane of thicker hair on the neck.

◀ LIFE-SIZE *Moose footprint*

Feeding Signs

As well as their trails, deer leave plenty of signs of their feeding activity if you know where to look. Check for signs of twigs and shoots torn off bushes and trees. Deer leave ragged tears where they have been feeding. Look for bark stripped from tree trunks. If a deer has been eating the bark, you will see long vertical marks and exposed wood where the animal has pulled off strips of bark. Large deer such as Moose may tear whole branches off trees or even knock small trees over entirely.

Caribou or Reindeer

SIZE Body: 7 ft (2.2 m); tail: 10 in (25 cm)
RANGE Alaska, Canada, Greenland, northern Europe, Asia
HABITAT Tundra and coniferous forest
FOOD Grass and leaves; also eats lichen and twigs in fall and winter
TRACKS AND SIGNS Caribou have broad, almost circular tracks about 3½ in (9 cm) wide, with the big dewclaws always showing. There is a large gap between the two cleaves.
COMMENTS In winter, lichen is an important food for Caribou, and you may spot scrape marks where the animal has dug into the snow to feed. Caribou is the only deer in which both male and female have antlers.

▲ Large deer can feed on branches up to 10 ft (3 m) high. This Elk is eating the leaves and acorns of an oak tree.

Cattle

▲ *A herd of African Buffalo move across the savanna. They are powerful animals that even the mighty Lion avoids.*

Cattle, such as cows and bison, belong to the bovid family, as do sheep, goats, and antelope. Cattle eat plants and live in North America, Africa, Europe, and Asia. In most species, both males and females have horns. They are even-toed and walk on their third and fourth toes, which form split, or cloven, hooves. The outer two toes, called dewclaws, are higher up the foot and do not reach the ground. Heavy cattle, such as cows, buffalo, and the Gaur, will leave clear tracks on softer ground. The front tracks are generally larger than the hind ones.

American Bison

COMMENTS Dried bison droppings burn well, and travelers used to use them as fuel for their fires.

SIZE Body: 11½ ft (3.5 m); tail: 24 in (60 cm)
RANGE North America, mostly in national parks and reserves; also now bred for food
HABITAT Grassland, open woodland
FOOD Mainly grass
TRACKS AND SIGNS This heavy animal, the largest in North America, leaves deep tracks 4–5 in (10–13 cm) wide that are usually easy to identify. The whole footprint is rounded, but each half, or cleave, is long and narrow with pointed tips.

Gaur

SIZE Body: 11 ft (3.4 m); tail: 3¼ ft (1 m)
RANGE India, Southeast Asia
HABITAT Hill forest
FOOD Mainly grass, but also leaves and stems
TRACKS AND SIGNS The Gaur is the largest ox, and its tracks, up to 5 in (12 cm) long, are easy to identify, as they are bigger than those of any other hoofed animal in the area.
COMMENTS The Gaur is very powerful and has big heavy horns. It has been known to turn on trackers and attack, so stay out of the way. Gaur live in small herds and are usually active at night.

Blue Wildebeest

SIZE Body: 8 ft (2.5 m); tail: 22 in (55 cm)
RANGE Africa: Kenya to northern South Africa
HABITAT Open grassland, usually near fresh water
FOOD Mainly grass
TRACKS AND SIGNS This wildebeest's narrow footprints are 4 in (10 cm) long. The front tracks are slightly curved, unlike those of the Black Wildebeest, and slightly larger than the hind tracks. Males often mark their territory by using their horns to gouge marks in the ground.
COMMENTS Wildebeest live in huge herds and travel long distances every year in search of water and fresh grass.

Tracker Signs

In bison or buffalo country, you may spot hollows in the ground where these huge animals have rolled in the dust or mud. This activity may bring the animals some relief from biting flies and other insects. In heavy rain, these wallows become temporary ponds. Look out for mud marks on nearby trees that the animal may have rubbed against and for hair caught in the bark. Bison droppings are large, up to 12 in (30 cm) long.

Herbivore Scats

The droppings of plant-eating animals, like those of meat eaters, can tell you a great deal about which animals are in an area and what they have been eating. Look at the size and shape of the dropping and note where you found it to help identification. Never handle any droppings you find with your bare hands.

Identifying droppings

Unlike meat eaters, which eat smaller amounts of a concentrated food, most plant eaters spend nearly all of their time eating in order to obtain enough nutrients. So, for their size, most plant eaters produce large amounts of scats. Some, such as sheep and rabbit scats, are small and round. Those of larger cattle, such as cows, bison, and buffalo, are a semiliquid mass that dries to form a flattened cake the size of a dinnerplate. The elephant produces up to 200 lbs (90 kg) of scats the size of a football every day. The color and texture of plant-eater scats varies with their diet. For example, deer droppings are softer and damper in summer, when the deer eat soft, lush leaves and grass. In winter, they eat tougher, more fibrous food and produce drier, firmer droppings.

Scent marking

Like carnivores, some plant eaters use their droppings to mark their territory. Rabbits, for example, leave large piles of droppings near their warren and around their territory. If another rabbit comes near, it will see and smell the droppings and know that the area is already taken.

Types of scats you might find

RABBITS AND HARES These are pellet-shaped scats made up of tough plant matter. Rabbit scats are almost round and measure about ½ in (1 cm) across. They vary from light brown to green or dark brown depending on diet. Hare scats are slightly larger and usually paler.

SQUIRRELS Squirrel scats are slightly smaller than rabbit scats, less round, and usually brownish in color. They contain plant matter and perhaps some insect remains.

BEAVERS Beaver scats are up to 1½ in (4 cm) long and about ¾ in (2 cm) thick. They contain very coarse fibrous plant matter as well as chips of wood and strips of bark.

DEER Deer scats are usually round or oval and often slightly pointed at one end. They are smooth, sometimes shiny, and contain plant remains. Those of larger deer, such as Moose, are up to 2 in (5 cm) long, while those of the smaller Elk are about 1 in (2.5 cm) long. In summer the scats are soft, damp, and may clump together.

SHEEP AND GOATS Sheep and goats leave scats in piles. Goat scats are about ½ in (1 cm) long, bean-shaped, and brownish; sheep scats are darker and rounder.

VOLES AND LEMMINGS These scats are brown or greenish and cylindrical. Water vole scats are about ½ in (1 cm) long; Norway Lemming scats are slightly smaller.

BIRDS The droppings of some birds are very liquid, while others produce long, round, or twisted droppings. Birds in a third group, including woodpeckers, leave firm, cylindrical droppings.

◄ *Elephant scats, like these, are large, barrel-shaped, and often left near water holes. They attract dung beetles, which feed on the dung and also lay their eggs in it.*

Identify the Animal

Eight of these droppings were left by plant-eating mammals—rabbit, squirrel, beaver, Elk, sheep, goat, water vole, and lemming. Two were left by birds—a woodpecker and a blackbird (a type of thrush). Can you guess which is which?

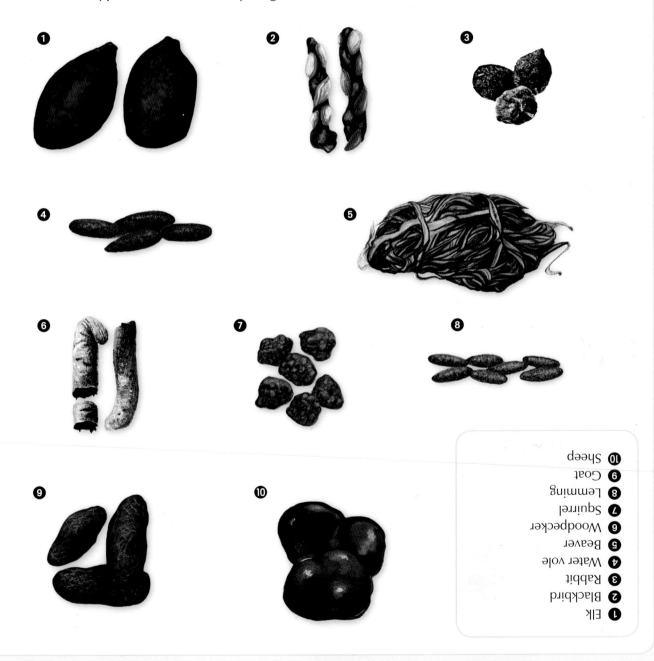

1 Elk
2 Blackbird
3 Rabbit
4 Water vole
5 Beaver
6 Woodpecker
7 Squirrel
8 Lemming
9 Goat
10 Sheep

Sheep and Goats

Wild sheep and goats are extremely nimble animals, able to climb rocky mountainsides and leap from ledge to ledge. They have four toes on each foot but walk on the two middle toes. The outside toes are called dewclaws. They live in remote areas, and their tracks are rarely seen except in snow.

▶ *The central parts of the hooves of this Mountain Goat are soft to help it grip rocky surfaces.*

Bighorn Sheep

SIZE Body: 6 ft (1.8 m); tail: 6 in (15 cm)
RANGE Canada, western U.S.A.
HABITAT Mountain slopes and high meadows
FOOD Grasses and other plants
TRACKS AND SIGNS The hoofprints of this sheep are about 3½ in (9 cm) long. They have straight outside edges and rounded tips.
COMMENTS Both males and females have horns, but those of males are much larger and curl around in a circle. Males fight fierce battles over who is to lead the herd.

Mountain Goat

SIZE Body: 5 ft (1.5 m); tail: 8 in (20 cm)
RANGE Western North America
HABITAT Rocky, mountainous areas
FOOD Grass, moss, lichens, woody plants
TRACKS AND SIGNS Hooves have a hard rim around a spongy central pad that helps the goat grip rocky surfaces. The tracks are about 2½ in (6.5 cm) long and similar to those of the Bighorn Sheep, but with more widely spread tips. There is usually a V-shaped gap between the tips. Trails of this animal are rarely seen, however, because they live in such high, remote places.
COMMENTS Males and females have short, dark horns.

Northern Chamois

SIZE Body: 4¼ ft (1.3 m); tail: 1½ in (4 cm)

RANGE Mountainous areas of southern, central, and eastern Europe, Turkey

HABITAT Rocky mountain slopes, alpine meadows

FOOD Green plants; moss and lichen in winter

TRACKS AND SIGNS The narrow tracks are 2¼ in (6 cm) long, with a gap between the two halves, or cleaves. In snow, or when the chamois is moving fast, the dewclaws often show in its tracks. Listen for the high-pitched whistling call that the chamois makes to warn others in the herd of danger.

COMMENTS Both males and females have slender horns that grow straight up and then bend back at the tip to make a hook shape.

Easy Tracking

You will find it easier to track a domestic sheep or goat than their wild relatives. The prints of domestic sheep (right) have a wide, squarish shape with rounded tips. Tracks of domestic goats are wider than those of wild goats. Each half, or cleave, is rounded at the end, and the dewclaws of domestic sheep and goats do not show.

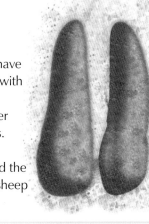

◄ *Unlike their wild relatives, domestic sheep tend to travel in groups, or flocks, while moving about in open country. If you find lots of sheep tracks together, they probably come from domestic sheep.*

Antelope and Pronghorn

Antelope are fast-moving, plant-eating mammals. All male and some female antelope have long horns, which are permanent. The Pronghorn of North America belongs to a separate family. Its horns are shed each year. Pronghorn and antelope have cloven hoofs, called cleaves, formed by the tips of their third and fourth toes.

▶ *The North American Pronghorn is now rare, due to hunting and the destruction of its habitat.*

Pronghorn

SIZE Body: 5 ft (1.5 m); tail: 7 in (18 cm)
RANGE Western North America from southern Canada to Mexico
HABITAT Grassland, desert
FOOD Grasses, leaves, cacti
TRACKS AND SIGNS The front tracks are up to 3¼ in (8 cm) long and are slightly larger than the hind tracks. The Pronghorn has no dewclaws. It nearly always trots or runs and seldom walks. Another sure sign of Pronghorns are the marks of the beds where they rest, usually in groups: a large oval area of flattened grass, in the open where the animal can easily spot any danger.
COMMENTS Pronghorns are the fastest-running animals in North America and can reach speeds of 60 mph (95 km/h).

Springbok

SIZE Body: 4½ ft (1.4 m); tail: 12 in (30 cm)
RANGE Southern Africa
HABITAT Dry savanna and semi-desert
FOOD Grass; also browses on bushes and trees in the dry season; may eat fruit such as melons
TRACKS AND SIGNS This antelope leaves a neat track about 2¼ in (6 cm) long, and both halves, or cleaves, have pointed tips. The hind foot is slightly larger than the front. It leaves piles of droppings to mark its territory.
COMMENTS The Springbok drinks water when it can, but it can last long periods without drinking as long as its food contains some water.

▲ *A Springbok leaps high into the air. The height it reaches shows any potential predator that this is no easy catch.*

Impala

SIZE Body: 5 ft
(1.5 m); tail: 16 in (40 cm)
RANGE Eastern Africa: Kenya
to northern South Africa
HABITAT Open woodland and
grassland, usually near water
FOOD Grass and leaves
TRACKS AND SIGNS The tracks of this antelope are
2 in (5 cm) long and show pointed toe prints, or
cleaves. The front and hind feet are about the same
size. Prints may be slightly blurred by tufts of hair on
the feet. Trails are often seen to and from water holes.
The male leaves piles of droppings in special places in
his territory during the mating season to alert females
to his presence.
COMMENTS Impala usually live in large
herds, led by dominant male
animals. Males mark their
territorial boundaries with urine
and droppings. Impala are fast
runners and can leap into the
air as they run.

The Springing Springbok

The Springbok gets its name from its habit of
making a series of bounds into the air, leaping as
high as 11½ ft (3.5 m). It holds its legs stiff and
straight as it bounds. The movement is called
"stotting" or "pronking" and may help to warn
others in the herd that predators are near. It may
also send a message to the predator that this is a
speedy, agile animal and the hunter should look
elsewhere for a meal.

▲ *In many parts of North Africa, camel trains such as this one in Somalia are still a very important form of transport.*

Camels

There are just four species in the camel family: the Bactrian (two-humped) Camel, the Dromedary (one-humped) Camel, and the Guanaco and Vicuña, both of which live in South America. Llamas and Alpacas are domestic animals, bred from the Guanaco for their thick wool. All these animals are plant eaters and can eat tough, even spiny, plants. A camel's humps are not for storing water, as people once thought, but for storing fat. This provides the camel with food when supplies are scarce in its desert home.

Bactrian Camel

SIZE Body: 11½ ft (3.5 m); tail: 20 in (50 cm)
RANGE Gobi Desert, Central Asia
HABITAT Desert and steppe
FOOD Grass, leaves, almost any plant
TRACKS AND SIGNS The Bactrian, like its relatives, has only two toes on each foot. The foot bones are expanded sideways as support for the broad flat pads on each foot, and there are nails on the upper surface of the toes. This foot structure stops the camel from sinking too deeply when it walks on soft, sandy soil, leaving tracks about 9 in (23 cm) wide.
COMMENTS The Bactrian has very long shaggy hair to keep it warm in the cold Gobi winter. In summer the hair is shed in large patches, leaving the animal's skin almost bare.

◄ SCALE: ¹/₆ *life-size*

Dromedary Camel

SIZE Body: 11½ ft (3.5 m); tail: 20 in (50 cm)
RANGE North Africa, Middle East; introduced in Australia
HABITAT Dry grassland, desert, plains
FOOD Plants, including tough, thorny bushes
TRACKS AND SIGNS Like the Bactrian, the Dromedary leaves splayed tracks up to 9 in (23 cm) wide and has feet adapted for walking on sand.
COMMENTS Dromedaries are now extinct in the wild, except in Australia, where there is a large feral (semi-wild) population. Domesticated camels are used as beasts of burden and for camel racing.

◄ SCALE: ¹/₆ *life-size*

▲ *A camel's feet are well adapted to walking on sand. They widen at the bottom, spreading the animal's weight over a large area, which prevents it from sinking.*

Desert Dweller

The Dromedary Camel is very well adapted to desert life. When going without food for long periods, it gets nutrients from fat reserves in its hump. When going without water, it can lose more than a quarter of its body weight yet remain healthy. When it finds water, it can drink up to 27 gallons (100 liters) in ten minutes to replace what it has lost. Its thick eyelashes protect its eyes from sand, and its small, narrow nostrils can close to keep out dust. Its body temperature drops at night and rises during the day, so it does not often need to sweat to cool itself—sweating uses water.

◄ LIFE-SIZE *footprint of Dromedary or Bactrian camel*

Vicuña

SIZE Body: 6 ft (1.8 m); tail: 10 in (25 cm)
RANGE Western South America: Peru and Chile
HABITAT High grassland
FOOD Grass and small plants
TRACKS AND SIGNS Like its relatives, the Vicuña has two toes on each foot, but its feet are smaller and narrower than those of camels. Listen for its alarm call, which is a clear whistling sound. Look for droppings, too. Vicuñas live in groups and usually leave their droppings in communal heaps to mark their territory.
COMMENTS The Vicuña has very fine but dense fur and often rolls in the dust to clean and scratch itself. You may see signs of this rolling activity on the ground.

Pigs and Peccaries

Wild pigs are stocky animals with big heads. They use their long snouts to root around on the ground for food, and most have sharp tusks. They all have four toes, the third and fourth of which form cloven (split) hooves. The smaller toes, called dewclaws, may or may not show in tracks. Peccaries are similar to pigs, but they are smaller and have tusks that point downward. Peccaries have only three toes on each back foot.

▲ Wild Boar are the ancestors of the domestic pig. Females live in groups, but males are usually found alone.

Collared Peccary

SIZE Body: 3¼ ft (1 m); tail: 2¼ in (5.5 cm)

RANGE Southwest U.S.A. to Argentina

HABITAT Very varied, including scrub and rain forest

FOOD Berries, roots, bulbs, cactus, fruit; also some snakes and small creatures such as worms and millipedes

TRACKS AND SIGNS These peccaries live in small groups and walk in single file as they move around in search of food. Their long cloven hooves leave trails that are 1½ in (4 cm) long. The dewclaws do not appear in tracks.

COMMENTS Active during the day, peccaries are shy animals. If approached by humans, they generally try to hide or run away, but if you get too close they can give savage bites.

Warthog

SIZE Body: 5 ft (1.5 m); tail: 20 in (50 cm)

RANGE Africa south of the Sahara

HABITAT Savanna, floodplain, light forest, open woodland

FOOD Plant material, including grass, berries, bark, roots; sometimes also eats carrion

TRACKS AND SIGNS This animal spends much time in muddy areas, where the tracks, 3¼ in (8 cm) long, are easy to see. Its hooves are quite narrow and the dewclaws sometimes show.

COMMENTS Warthogs sometimes dig their own burrows, or they may use those left by other animals such as the Aardvark or porcupines. They may take in dry grass as bedding for young, and you may spot this around the entrance.

Wild Boar

SIZE Body: 6 ft (1.8 m); tail: 12 in (30 cm)

RANGE Europe, North Africa, Asia; introduced in Australia, New Zealand, U.S.A., South America

HABITAT Woodland, forest, wetlands

FOOD Plant material, including nuts, roots, bulbs; also eats insects and carrion

TRACKS AND SIGNS The tracks, up to 2½ in (6.5 cm) wide, usually show clear dewclaw marks, whether the boar is walking or running. The toe (cleave) marks are broad and rounded.

COMMENTS Most Wild Boar make a nest of some sort. They usually prefer to avoid humans, but if they are cornered, their sharp tusks make them dangerous.

Wallowing

Wild pigs, such as Wild Boar and Warthogs, love to wallow in mud. This helps to cool the animals down in hot weather and also controls biting insects and parasites. When the mud dries on the skin, it provides some protection against the sun, acting like a natural sunblock. Warthogs and Wild Boar may appear very different colors according to the type of mud in their area. Telltale signs that there are wild pigs nearby include streaks of mud on tree trunks where an animal has rubbed itself after wallowing.

▼ *Warthogs and other wild pigs love to wallow in muddy pools. Look for tracks at wallows and signs of them rubbing against the surrounding trees.*

Whales, Dolphins, and Seals

Whales, dolphins, and seals are all marine mammals with flippers and fins instead of legs. They must still breathe air, however, and seals have to come to land to give birth to their young. Whales and dolphins spend all their lives in water. You can see seals on land quite easily, but to spot whales you must watch for signs of their activity, such as flipper and fins above the surface, and signs of disturbance in the water.

▲ *Humpback Whales sometimes leap out of the water, or breach. They are most likely to do this when they are in groups, so breaching may be a form of communication.*

Common Dolphin

SIZE Length: 8 ft (2.4 m)
RANGE Worldwide, temperate and tropical oceans
HABITAT Coastal and open ocean
FOOD Fish and squid
SIGNS Dolphins never come onto land and so cannot leave tracks, but there are various signs to look out for. You may spot the back fin above the water. It is about 16 in (40 cm) tall and has a curved shape. Dolphins also often travel in a series of leaps and dives and they often bowride behind a ship, frolicking in the waves.
COMMENTS This dolphin has distinctive yellowish and gray markings on its sides, which make it very easy to recognize.

Humpback Whale

SIZE Length: 50 ft (15 m)
RANGE All oceans
HABITAT Coastal waters and open ocean
FOOD Fish and krill (shrimplike creatures)
SIGNS The Humpback's blow (see opposite page) is about 10 ft (3 m) high. The Humpback often leaps clear of the surface in a spectacular backward flip or lies at the surface with one of its long flippers held up in the air.
COMMENTS The easiest way to recognize this whale is by its side (pectoral) flippers, which are the longest of any whale. The flippers have knobbly uneven edges and, at about 15 ft (5 m) long, are about a third of the length of the whale's body.

Common Seal

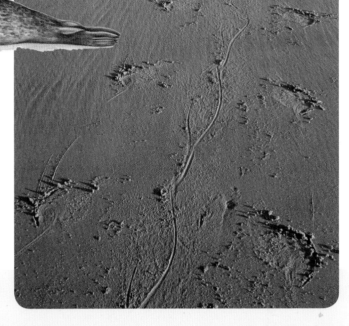

SIZE Length: 6 ft (1.8 m)

RANGE North Atlantic, North Pacific, Arctic Ocean

HABITAT Coastal waters and estuaries

FOOD Fish

TRACKS AND SIGNS Like all seals, the Common Seal often comes onto land to bask on rocks and beaches. It also mates and gives birth on land. You may see a seal's trail in the sand where it has heaved its body along with its flippers. When you're on the coast, keep a look out for the seal's whiskered nose bobbing at the water's surface.

COMMENTS Hundreds of seals gather on beaches in the breeding season. They return to the same beach each year. The females come ashore to give birth in February farther south, and as late as July in Arctic regions. Common Seals often gather around harbors and are sometimes known as Harbor Seals.

▲ *Seals leave a distinctive track as they haul themselves along on muddy or sandy beaches. A trail is left by the seal's body, which remains close to the ground, with prints of the flippers to each side.*

Whale Blows

Even when a whale comes to the surface of the sea to take a breath, most of its body stays below the water. If you are very lucky you may see a whale breach (leap clear of the water) or see a tail or fin above the surface. But the most likely sign to spot is the whale blow—the cloud of vapor in the air as it breathes out. Different species have differently shaped blows. Some spout straight up, while others are at an angle. Some whales, such as the Black Right Whale, have two spouts, while others have only one.

▶ *This Fin Whale has one blowhole in the top of its head, through which it blows misty air straight up above the sea.*

Hyrax, Elephant Shrew, and Aardvark

These three creatures are all oddities. Elephant shrews are a small family of 15 insect-eating animals. There is just one species of Aardvark, also an insect eater. It has a long snout for rooting out its prey. The four species of hyrax look like large guinea pigs, but they have feet with flattened nails like hooves.

◄ *A Rock Hyrax catches some morning sun to warm its body temperature after a cold night in the scrub.*

Rock Hyrax

SIZE Body: 24 in (60 cm); tail: none
RANGE Africa south of the Sahara
HABITAT Rocky scrub
FOOD Grasses and other plants

TRACKS AND SIGNS The tracks are about 2 in (5 cm) long but may be difficult to find as this animal often moves around on rocky surfaces. It has four short, wide toes on the front feet and three on the hind. A special curved grooming claw on the inside toe on each hind foot usually shows in tracks. On the underside of each foot is a sticky moist cup that helps the hyrax grip rocks. You may also see marks where the hyrax has dragged its bottom along the ground.
COMMENTS Hyraxes cannot control their body temperature very well and are often seen sunning themselves on rocks to warm up. If startled, they run into a burrow or rock crevice.

Short-eared Elephant Shrew

SIZE Body: 4 in (10 cm); tail: 5 in (13 cm)
RANGE Southern Africa
HABITAT Dry bush
FOOD Ants and termites, but also eats some plant roots, shoots, and berries

TRACKS AND SIGNS These little animals leave small light tracks that may be spotted in the sand. Their feet have five toes but only four generally show in the tracks, which are about $1/3$ in (7 mm) long.
COMMENTS Elephant shrews are neither elephants nor shrews. They are so-called because they look a little like shrews, although they have longer legs, and they have trunk-like noses like elephants do, only much shorter.

◄ LIFE-SIZE *footprint*

▶ SCALE: *5 x life-size track of Short-eared Elephant Shrew*

Smash and Grab

The Aardvark is specially equipped for feeding on insects, and you may see signs of its digging activity. Using its strong legs and huge hooflike claws, the Aardvark can dig at tremendous speed to uncover an underground ants' nest or break open a termite mound. Once its prey is exposed, the Aardvark laps up huge numbers with its extraordinary tongue. This tongue is up to 18 in (45 cm) long and is covered with sticky saliva. Large numbers of insects stick to the tongue each time it is flicked into the nest, and they are then crushed by the Aardvark's broad teeth. The Aardvark can close off its nostrils and ears when digging so they do not get filled with dust.

▶ *An Aardvark digs into a termite mound.*
Its long claws make it an expert digger.

Aardvark

SIZE Body: 4 ft (1.2 m); tail: 22 in (55 cm)
RANGE Africa south of the Sahara
HABITAT Grassland, bush, woodland, preferably where there is sandy soil
FOOD Ants and termites are the main food, but Aardvarks may also catch other insects
TRACKS AND SIGNS The Aardvark has strong feet with four toes on the front feet and five on the hind. All the toes have very large, broad, hooflike claws. Only three toes usually show in the tracks, sometimes with the tips of other claws. The front prints are around 3¼ in (8.5 cm) long, the hind prints slightly larger.

Ⓗ

Aardvaark claws leave deep marks in the ground where the animal has dug for insects.
COMMENTS This animal digs a burrow with a very wide entrance that is easy to spot. You may notice deep grooves made by the Aardvark's claws in the sides of the burrow entrance.

Moles and Shrews

Moles, hedgehogs, and shrews are small mammals that live on the ground and feed mostly on insects and other small creatures such as worms. Many of them have long narrow snouts for reaching into small spaces to find their prey. They also have sharp teeth and claws. Moles leave plenty of signs of their activity, including tunnels and molehills.

◄ *Hedgehog droppings are usually hard and dark in color. They contain material such as insect wings, shells, and sometimes the bones of small vertebrates. They are up to 2 in (5 cm) long and tubular in shape.*

European Mole

SIZE Body: 6¼ in (16 cm); tail: ¾ in (2 cm)
RANGE Europe, western Asia
HABITAT Forest, fields, scrub
FOOD Earthworms and other small creatures as well as snakes, lizards, and mice
TRACKS AND SIGNS Mole tracks are very rarely seen, since these animals spend nearly all of their time underground. But if tracks do appear, the prints made by the hind feet will be about ¾ in (2 cm) long and will show five toes tipped with long claws. The front feet are adapted for digging and cannot be placed flat on the ground, so in the tracks they leave, only the claws are visible.
COMMENTS When a mole digs its tunnels, it pushes up piles of earth on the surface. Called molehills, these are a sure sign of moles in an area.

European Hedgehog

SIZE Body: 10 in (25 cm);
tail: 1¼ in (3 cm)
RANGE Western Europe; introduced in New Zealand
HABITAT Forest, farmland
FOOD Hedgehogs root around in hedges and underground for insects and other small creatures
TRACKS AND SIGNS Hedgehogs have five clawed toes on each foot, and all these usually show on tracks. The front and hind tracks are roughly the same size at about 1¼ in (3 cm) long. Look too for the hedgehog's shiny black droppings, in which you can usually see insect remains, such as wings, and sometimes bits of fur and feathers.
COMMENTS If in danger, the hedgehog curls itself up into a prickly ball, which makes it very difficult for predators to attack.

Star-nosed Mole

This extraordinary mole has 22 fingerlike tentacles around its nose. These are very sensitive, and the mole uses them to search for food on the bottom of ponds and streams. This mole is an excellent swimmer and diver and feeds mostly on water-dwelling creatures such as shellfish, fish, and aquatic insects. Its tracks are rarely seen, but look for piles of mud left when the Star-nosed Mole digs its burrow near streams and rivers.

▲ *A Star-nosed Mole emerges from the undergrowth. It is almost totally blind, so it relies on the 22 sensitive tentacles on the end of its nose to identify prey, which includes worms, insects, and crustaceans.*

Masked Shrew

SIZE Body: 4 in (10 cm); tail: 3 in (7.5 cm)
RANGE North America
HABITAT Forest, marshes, damp fields, woodland
FOOD Earthworms, snails, and other small creatures
TRACKS AND SIGNS This little creature bounds around in search of food, and since it likes to live in moist areas, its tracks are often seen. It has five toes on each foot, and all generally appear in its tracks. The front tracks are only about ¼ in (5 mm) long, but the back ones are larger—over ½ in (1.5 cm) long. Sometimes a mark of the shrew's tail is also seen in tracks.

COMMENTS Despite its small size, the Masked Shrew has a large appetite and gobbles up huge numbers of insects and other creatures, often eating more than its own body weight every day.

◀ LIFE-SIZE *footprint*

▲ SCALE: *5 x life-size track of Masked Shrew*

Mammal Nests

Many animals sleep above the ground in trees or bushes, most of them just curling up on a branch or in a tree hole. Some primates, though, including chimpanzees and gorillas, make sleeping platforms by weaving branches together. And a few mammal species make nests that look like bird nests and are made of similar materials, such as twigs, leaves, and other plant material. These mammals include squirrels, harvest mice, and dormice. If you see what might be the nest of a small mammal, never go too near unless you are sure it has been abandoned.

Squirrel nests

Tree squirrels usually have several nests where they sleep, hide away from enemies, and rear their young. Some nests may be simply a hole in a tree, but squirrels also make ball-shaped nests of leaves and twigs high up in trees. The nest is made of twigs woven together and is lined with grass and moss. Squirrels do not hibernate, but in cold weather they may spend much time in the nest. Young squirrels are born blind, naked, and helpless, and do not venture out of the nest until they are about six weeks old. Their mother keeps the nest clean and changes the bedding material regularly.

◀ A Eurasian Red Squirrel has made this nest high up in the safety of a pine tree.

▲ One of the places the Eurasian Harvest Mouse likes to make its nests is in corn fields, often near ditches at the edge, and they also like to nest in reed beds.

Dormouse nest

A dormouse's summer nest, where it rears its young, is usually made a short distance above the ground. It is made of hay, moss, bark fibers, and other plant material woven into a round or oval shape and lined with shredded grass. The dormouse is active at night and spends the day asleep in its nest. The dormouse also needs a safe place for its long winter hibernation. This nest may be made on the ground or in a tree hole. The dormouse will also use wooden nest boxes provided by humans on tree trunks for its winter sleep, which can last until April or May.

◀ A dormouse sleeps right through the cold winter in the safety of its nest.

How the Eurasian Harvest Mouse Makes Its Nest

The little Eurasian Harvest Mouse makes its summer nest on tall reeds or grass stems, low down in a tree or bush in hedgerows, or at the edge of a field. She makes the nest for her young shortly before they are born. The mouse gives birth in the nest, and her young stay there for about three weeks. A winter nest is made on the ground or among plant roots.

❶ *The mouse chooses suitable grass or reed stems then winds the leaves of one stem around another to make a platform.*

❷ *She then cuts more pieces of grass, which she splits with her teeth and uses to weave the walls of the nest.*

❸ *Gradually she builds a neat ball-shaped nest that measures about 4 in (10 cm) across.*

❹ *She then weaves more grass into the outer wall.*

Beaver, Nutria, and Paca

These animals are among the largest of the rodent family, and they all live near water. Beavers build elaborate dams and lodges in which to live and store food, while Nutrias and Pacas dig burrows for shelter. Like all rodents, these animals have very strong, sharp front teeth, which keep growing throughout their lives. A beaver can cut through a tree trunk in minutes to get wood for its building activities.

▶ *Beavers use their sharp teeth to fell trees. Pointed tree stumps are a sure sign that there are beavers nearby.*

North American Beaver

SIZE Body: 32 in (80 cm); tail: 18 in (45 cm)
RANGE North America, except desert regions and northern Canada; introduced in France, Poland, Finland, Russia
HABITAT Streams, ponds, and lakes in wooded areas
FOOD Bark, twigs, leaves, roots, water plants
TRACKS AND SIGNS The tracks of this beaver, like those of its European cousin, are quite easy to identify. The hind track is up to 6 in (15 cm) long, the front about 3½ in (9 cm). There are five toes on each foot. The front tracks show four or five toes, the hind tracks five. The hind feet are also webbed. In snow, the tail may leave a trail.
COMMENTS Beavers cut down trees and gnaw off branches to build dams and lodges. They leave small piles of twigs and earth around their territory.

Ⓗ

▶ SCALE: ¼ *life-size*

Nutria or Coypu

SIZE Body: 24 in (60 cm); tail: 18 in (45 cm)
RANGE South America; introduced in North America, Europe, Asia
HABITAT Near marshes, lakes, streams
FOOD Water plants are the Nutria's main food, but it also eats grass
TRACKS AND SIGNS Nutria tracks usually show five toes on each foot and long claws. The hind feet have webbing between four toes. The hind print is up to 6 in (15 cm) long and much larger than the front. You may also see the mark of the long tail dragging on the ground. Its small droppings are found near streams.
COMMENTS This large rodent is a native of South America. It is farmed elsewhere for its fur. Many animals have escaped and now breed in Ⓗ their new habitats.

◀ SCALE: ¼ *life-size*

◀ LIFE-SIZE *footprint of North American Beaver*

▶ LIFE-SIZE *footprint of Nutria*

A Beaver Lodge

When a family of beavers moves into an area, it makes far-reaching changes. The family begins by damming a stream, using branches, tree trunks, and mud to create a quiet area of water where they can build their lodge. The dam also makes a storage area for winter food. The beavers cut extra branches in the fall and store them under water near the dam. The lodge, too, is built from branches and plastered with mud. The entrance is below the water surface well away from predators. The beaver's work is never finished. It constantly has to repair the dam and lodge, adding more mud, twigs, and sticks.

▼ A North American Beaver busies itself with repairs to a dam. The important work of maintaining the dam is shared by the whole family group.

Paca

SIZE Body: 30 in (75 cm); tail: 1¼ in (3 cm)
RANGE Southern Mexico to northern Argentina
HABITAT Forest near water
FOOD Leaves, roots, seeds; also eats fallen fruits such as avocados
TRACKS AND SIGNS Another large stocky rodent, the Paca often leaves well-used trails and clear tracks on muddy riverbanks. It has four toes on the front feet and five on the hind. The hind tracks are usually slightly larger than the front tracks, which are about 1¾ in (4.5 cm) wide. Other signs of the Paca are burrows in the riverbank or among tree roots. Each burrow may have several exits just in case.
COMMENTS Pacas are good swimmers and often run for the water when in danger. They are usually active at night. They may bury seeds when food is plentiful and dig them up when they need them.

Rats and Mice

Rats and mice are some of the world's most successful mammals, and hundreds of species live in many different habitats. The secret of their success is their adaptability—they eat almost anything and can live almost anywhere. Some rats and mice generally live near humans, where they know they will always have food supplies. Rats and mice are also important prey animals for many other kinds of creatures.

◀ *A Brown Rat feeds in the undergrowth. It comes out to forage at night and will eat almost anything.*

Brown Rat

SIZE Body: 11 in (28 cm); tail: 9 in (23 cm)
RANGE Originally Asia but now worldwide

HABITAT Everywhere, usually near humans
FOOD Seeds, fruits, leaves; also small animals, scraps
TRACKS AND SIGNS The Brown Rat has four toes on the front feet and five on the hind feet, all of which usually show in its tracks. The front tracks are about 1 in (2.5 cm) wide. The hind feet are longer, measuring about 2 in (5 cm). As it bounds along, the Brown Rat leaves groups of four prints. Rats and mice often pass urine as they run, so look for streaks of urine near trails.
COMMENTS The Brown Rat is one of the most widespread and common animals of all. It is a burrower and may disturb foundations by digging under buildings.

House Mouse

SIZE Body: up to 4 in (10 cm); tail: 4 in (10 cm)
RANGE Originally Asia but now worldwide
HABITAT Very varied, usually near humans
FOOD Seeds, grain, human foods
TRACKS AND SIGNS
Tracks of this little creature are seen only in soft surfaces, such as snow or mud. Where they do appear, tracks are under ½ in (15 mm) long, and show four toes on front feet and five on back feet. The tail may appear in trails in snow. Look for small round droppings near tracks and feeding places.
COMMENTS Like the Brown Rat, the House Mouse is extremely common and can do great damage to stored food, being able to chew through tough bags and packaging.

Deer Mouse

SIZE Body: up to 4 in (10 cm); tail: 4 in (10 cm)
RANGE North America
HABITAT Forest, grassland, scrub
FOOD Seeds, nuts, berries, fruit; also insects, other small creatures, and carrion

TRACKS AND SIGNS These little mice are generally active at night so you are not likely to spot them, but you may see their tracks on soft surfaces, such as mud or snow. Its tracks are very like those of the House Mouse, but these mice are less likely to be around human homes. The tail may show in trails in the snow.

COMMENTS Deer Mice are extremely common and will live in almost any kind of habitat with sufficient food. They may find their way into sheds or other buildings for protection during winter.

Food Pests

Like all rodents, rats and mice have sharp teeth and can chew their way through wood and wire, as well as cloth bags and other storage materials. They can also climb well and jump. Once they get access to stores, rats and mice not only eat the food but also spoil vast amounts with their droppings and urine. They carry a number of serious diseases, such as rabies, so it is not safe to eat food that rats and mice have spoiled. With a plentiful food supply, rats and mice reproduce rapidly, hugely increasing the amount of damage they can wreak. Females can bear several litters of 20 or more young in a single year.

95

Mammals

▼ *Rats can destroy grain supplies and will reproduce very quickly, so that within a few weeks there may be thousands of them feasting on the stores.*

Squirrels

Squirrels are a type of rodent, and there are at least 260 different species. These include tree squirrels, such as the Gray Squirrel and Red Squirrel, species that spend more time on the ground, such as chipmunks, and others that dig underground burrows, such as prairie dogs and Groundhogs. Most are active during the day and have good eyesight. Plant matter, including nuts, seeds, and fruit, is their main food, but most squirrels will eat insects and other small creatures from time to time. Many are quite easy to see if you watch patiently.

▲ *This North American Red Squirrel is eating a pine cone. Chewed cones and nut shells on the ground are common signs of squirrels.*

Eastern Gray Squirrel

SIZE Body: 11 in (28 cm); tail: 10 in (25 cm)
RANGE Eastern North America; introduced in western North America, South Africa, Great Britain, parts of continental Europe
HABITAT Forest, woodland
FOOD Nuts, acorns, seeds, buds, fruit; occasionally eats insects and birds' eggs
TRACKS AND SIGNS The front tracks are about 1 in (2.5 cm) long and show four toes. The hind feet are twice as long and show five toes. Squirrels generally jump along on the ground, and their trails show sets of four prints about 2 in (5 cm) long. You may also spot lots of feeding signs, including acorn shells, partly chewed pine cones on the ground, and chewed bark.
COMMENTS Like most tree squirrels, this species either builds a nest from twigs wedged into the fork of a branch or else nests in a tree hole.

Ⓗ

Eastern Chipmunk

SIZE Body: 7 in (18 cm); tail: 5 in (13 cm)
RANGE Eastern North America
HABITAT Forest and woodland
FOOD Nuts, acorns, seeds, fungi, corn, fruit; also eats insects, other small creatures, birds' eggs
TRACKS AND SIGNS Chipmunks are quite easy to spot

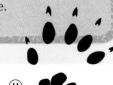

in the wild, and you may see them gathering food or hear their chirping, birdlike calls. Their tracks are not easy to find, as chipmunks are very light. If you do see prints, the front ones will be about 1 in (2.5 cm) long and show four toes; the hind feet are about twice that length with five toes.
COMMENTS Chipmunks spend much of their time on the ground but will scamper up trees to escape predators or get food. They live in burrows, which they dig under rocks or logs, and store food in summer to last them through the winter.

Ⓗ

Groundhog or Woodchuck

SIZE Body: 32 in (80 cm); tail: 6 in (15 cm)
RANGE Canada, eastern U.S.A.
HABITAT Woods and grassland
FOOD Grasses, leaves, fruit, grains, roots, some insects
TRACKS AND SIGNS Groundhogs are much heavier than most squirrels and more likely to leave clear tracks, which are very similar to those of tree squirrels—four toes on the front feet and five on the hind feet—but much larger, up to 2¾ in (7 cm) long. When walking, the Groundhog's hind footprints usually overlap the front. Another sign of the Groundhog is its burrow, which may have wide openings and deep tunnels and contains a special area for droppings.
COMMENTS The Groundhog is usually active during the day and is quite easy to see if you do not scare it away. If a Groundhog senses danger, it may sit up on its back legs to look around.

Prairie Dogs

Prairie dogs are a kind of ground-living squirrel. They make a sharp, doglike bark if threatened and to warn others in their group of danger. Large groups of them live in huge underground burrows, called towns, which contain many tunnels and chambers. Other creatures may find places to live in the towns, including predators of prairie dogs such as burrowing owls and snakes. Prairie dogs come out in the daytime to feed on grass. They live in the western United States and Mexico. They used to be very common, but huge numbers have been killed by humans because they damage crops and pasture.

▲ *The Norway Lemming leaves many small, pale-colored droppings less than ¼ in (6 mm) long. They are found in open grassy areas, and near burrows, often in large heaps.*

Voles and Lemmings

Voles and lemmings are rodents that live in North America, Europe, and Asia. They are mostly small creatures with a stocky body, short legs, and small ears close to the head. They feed mainly on plants and usually live in groups. Some, such as water voles and the Muskrat, live near water and can swim. It is rare to see clear trails, except in snow, but there are plenty of other signs you can look for.

Meadow Vole

SIZE Body: 5 in (12 cm); tail: 2½ in (6.5 cm)
RANGE Canada and northern U.S.A.
HABITAT Grassland and woodland, often near streams and rivers
FOOD Plants, including grass, seeds, roots, and bark
TRACKS AND SIGNS There are lots of vole species, and it is difficult to tell these small light animals apart by their tracks, which are similar and often faint. When tracks are found, they are about ½ in (1.5 cm) long and show four toes on the front feet and five on the hind. The surest sign of vole activity is the little runways of trimmed grass they make in their territory, along which you will see piles of droppings.

COMMENTS In winter, voles run around in tunnels they make under the snow. You may see little round openings to these tunnels.

Ⓗ

Muskrat

SIZE Body: 13 in (33 cm); tail: 12 in (30 cm)
RANGE North America; introduced in northern Eurasia
HABITAT Marshland, lakes, ponds, rivers
FOOD Water and land plants; small amount of fish and shellfish in some areas
TRACKS AND SIGNS The Muskrat spends much time in water, but its tracks are easily found on riverbanks. It often lives near beavers, but its footprints are much smaller. The hind tracks are about 2¾ in (7 cm) long—twice as long as the front—and usually show all five toes. There are small webs between the toes of the hind feet. You may also see marks from the tail where it drags on the ground.
COMMENTS Look for the Muskrat's small, often green, pellet-shaped droppings. These are left in piles to mark the Muskrat's territory. Do not go too near these—any disturbance to them may cause the Muskrat to leave the area.

Ⓗ

Muskrat Homes

Muskrats are not quite such amazing builders as beavers, but they do make very interesting homes. Some Muskrats dig burrows in riverbanks. The burrow may have several entrances below water level and a tunnel leading to a nesting chamber. Muskrats also build nests, rather like beaver lodges, in the water. The house is made of reeds, grass, and mud and the underwater entrance enables the animal to come and go without being seen by predators. It is kept very clean outside. Droppings, food remains, and other trash are left on nearby logs and rocks. Muskrats also take their food to a feeding platform, a floating raft they make from mud, reeds, and sticks, where they can sit and eat in safety, well away from any predators on the riverbank.

Norway Lemming

SIZE Body: 5 in (12 cm); tail: 1 in (2.5 cm)
RANGE Scandinavia eastward to Russia
HABITAT Tundra and grassland
FOOD Grasses, shrubs, moss
TRACKS AND SIGNS The tracks are ¾ in (2 cm) wide, with four front toes and five hind. Lemmings roll from side to side as they walk, so the tracks will do the same.
COMMENTS Every few years the population of this species explodes. Look for droppings (see opposite) along the trails to its burrows and, in snowy areas, for entrances to lemming runways beneath the snow.

▲ *Water voles have special places called latrines where they leave their droppings. Latrines are often on a riverbank, as is the case with this European Water Vole. The droppings are cylindrical, with rounded ends and up to ½ in (1.5 cm) long.*

Rabbits and Hares

Rabbits and hares are fast-running animals with powerful back legs. They have long ears—and excellent hearing—and very short tails. They feed on plants and have strong teeth for gnawing through tough stalks. These animals can live happily in a wide variety of habitats. Some species, such as the European Rabbit, have been introduced around the world and have spread rapidly. Hare and rabbit tracks are similar, but those of hares are bigger. Pikas are smaller relatives of rabbits and hares. They have short rounded ears and no visible tail.

▲ *This European Rabbit latrine (an area where droppings are regularly left) is highly visible and marks out territory.*

Brown Hare

SIZE Body: 27 in (68 cm); tail: 4 in (10 cm)
RANGE Europe, Asia; introduced in North and South America, Australia, New Zealand
HABITAT Open country, farmland, woodland
FOOD Grass, buds, leaves; also twigs and bark when green food is scarce
TRACKS AND SIGNS Hares leave pointed front tracks about 2 in (5 cm) long. The front feet have five toes, but the fifth rarely shows in tracks. The hind feet are twice as long as the front and their four toes all show in tracks. The thick hair on the soles of the feet may also show in the tracks. The greater the distance between the prints, the faster the animal is traveling. Look for feeding signs, such as gnawing marks on trees.
COMMENTS Hares do not make burrows but simply scrape a little hollow in the ground and lie down to sleep. The hollow, called a form, is tricky to spot, but you may notice a small, flattened area near a clump of grass or rock. It is easiest to spot in snow.

Desert Cottontail

SIZE Body: 15 in (38 cm); tail: 2¼ in (6 cm)
RANGE Western U.S.A. and Mexico
HABITAT Dry open areas and sagebrush
FOOD Plants, twigs, bark
TRACKS AND SIGNS Like the Brown Hare, the Desert Cottontail has five toes on the front feet but four on the hind. The hind tracks are about 3 in (7.5 cm) long. The prints may be unclear because the soles of the feet are covered with thick, springy hair. Cottontails hop a lot, and the trail shows as groups of four prints. The droppings, which are small and pellet-shaped, usually brown with traces of grass and other plants, are often left on logs and tree stumps.
COMMENTS Rarely digs burrows, but may use burrows of other animals or sleep in dips in the ground, where you may see trails. This species also climbs trees.

(H)

Seasonal Colors

The Snowshoe Hare has two coats—one for winter and one for summer. In summer, this hare has a reddish brown or gray coat. But in winter, it molts, shedding the dark hair and growing a new coat of white fur, making the animal very difficult to see in the snow. The color change is triggered by the change in day length, not the weather. So if the snow is late in arriving, the hare might find itself gleaming white against the brown earth. In fall and spring, you may spot hares with a mixture of the two colors as the coat changes.

▶ *As winter turns to spring, the Snowshoe Hare's fur coat changes from white (above) to brown (below).*

European Rabbit

SIZE Body: 18 in (46 cm); tail: 3 in (8 cm)

RANGE Europe, northwest Africa; introduced in South America, Australia, New Zealand, and many other islands

HABITAT Grassland, farmland, wooded areas

FOOD Grass and other green plants; also twigs and bark

TRACKS AND SIGNS Tracks look like those of the hare but are smaller—the hind foot is about 1½ in (4 cm) long. There will also be a shorter distance between the groups of footprints. Look for signs of feeding, such as bark gnawed up from the base to a short distance above ground, and neat, clean cuts where the rabbit has bitten off twigs.

COMMENTS This rabbit does dig burrows. Look for little mounds of earth near the entrances.

Feeding Signs FRUIT, NUTS, AND CONES

Fruits, nuts, and seeds are all very important foods for a wide range of animals and contain much more protein and other nutrients than leaves do. Their popularity is good for the plants, too. The animals disperse the seeds either by eating them and pooping them out or by burying them and then forgetting about them. Animals leave plenty of signs of their feeding activities. Look out for chewed cones, nutshells, and partly eaten fruit. Badgers often leave half-eaten bulbs on the ground, and voles make underground stores of food.

Fruit

Fruit and berries are an important food for many animals, ranging from huge bears to tiny mice. When large animals eat fruit, they gobble it up whole and the only sign will be in the droppings. Some smaller animals may eat only the flesh of the fruit, while others extract the kernels. Squirrels generally prefer the flesh, and you may find a pile of cherry pits under trees where they feed. Mice and voles prefer the pits, and you will see fine tooth marks on the edges.

◄ Squirrels may store food in hiding places to provide a supply when food is scarce. These apples have been wedged between tree branches by a North American Red Squirrel.

Nuts

Nuts such as walnuts and hazelnuts are a very rich food and popular with many animals, including squirrels, mice, voles, and birds. But first, the animal has to break through the nut's thick shell. A squirrel gnaws an opening into the nut and then sticks in its big lower front teeth and breaks open the shell. If you see split open shells or pieces of shell on the ground, you will know a squirrel has been feeding. Mice and voles hold the nut and scrape away with their teeth until they make a hole. They then feed by extracting bits of the kernel with their big lower teeth. Look for empty shells with neat holes gnawed in them.

Cones

Lots of animals, including squirrels, rodents, and birds, feed on the seeds, or pine nuts, in pine cones. They gnaw away the outer scales that protect the seeds to get at their tasty meal. Small rodents, such as mice and voles, nibble away at cones until they can get no more food. What is left looks very neat and clean. Squirrels are larger, with stronger teeth. They tear off scales, leaving cones with ragged, frayed edges.

▼ These pine cone remains show two cores from which squirrels have torn off the surrounding piles of scales in order to get at the nutritious seeds inside.

Fungi

Many animals feed on fungi, particularly in fall. Some fungi are large, and an animal may eat part of it and leave the rest. Look for the large tooth marks of squirrels and small teeth marks of voles and mice. Some birds peck at fungi in search of fungus grubs, leaving holes made by their beak.

◄ *Toothmarks on the top of this mushroom cap show where it has been gnawed at by a small rodent.*

Identifying the Signs

The remains of the cones and hazelnuts below have been left by either squirrels or deer mice. Can you tell which is which?

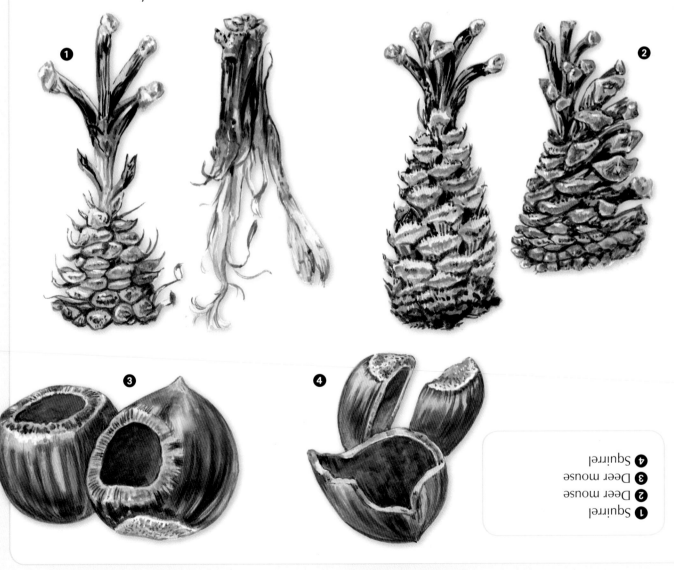

❶ Squirrel
❷ Deer mouse
❸ Deer mouse
❹ Squirrel

Porcupines

Porcupines are large rodents with long, sharp, loosely attached spines, called quills, on their backs and tails. They live in Africa, Asia, and North and South America. African and Asian species live mostly on the ground. American species spend much of their time in trees and their feet have strong claws and pebbly soles to give a good grip. If threatened, porcupines raise their quills to make themselves look bigger and may rattle the quills and thrash their spiny tails around. Some species will also charge backward to drive their quills into the enemy.

▲ *Porcupines make their dens in caves, hollow trees, or, as here, decaying logs. Droppings surround the entrance.*

North American Porcupine

SIZE Body: 32 in (80 cm);
tail: 12 in (30 cm)
RANGE North America: Alaska to Mexico
HABITAT Tundra, forest, scrub
FOOD Leaves, roots, flowers, seeds, bark, conifer needles
TRACKS AND SIGNS This large rodent has sharp quills to protect it and so it rarely runs. There are four toes on the front feet, five on the hind feet, and the tracks are easy to recognize because they have long claw marks and the soles have a pebbly surface. The hind tracks are up to 4½ in (11.5 cm) long, the front up to 3 in (7.5 cm) long. The tracks point inward and you may see marks of the tail dragging along.
COMMENTS Look for chewed bark and twigs under trees—often a sign of porcupine activity. You may also see piles of droppings under trees.

Crested Porcupine

SIZE Body: 32 in (80 cm);
tail: 5 in (12.5 cm)
RANGE North and sub-Saharan East and Central Africa; introduced in Italy
HABITAT Varied: forest, grassland, rocky scrub
FOOD Bulbs, roots, fruit, bark; some insects
TRACKS AND SIGNS This is the largest African rodent, with prints up to 3¼ in (8 cm) long. The front and hind prints show four toes and claws—there are five toes on the front feet but the first is very small and doesn't always show on tracks. The tracks are sometimes mistaken for those of the Honey Badger (see pages 34–35), but the porcupine's claws are much shorter.
COMMENTS Look for quills, which may drop out as the animal moves around.

Tree Porcupine

SIZE Body: 24 in (60 cm); tail: 20 in (50 cm)

RANGE Northeast South America

HABITAT Tropical forest

FOOD Leaves, stems, fruit, bark

TRACKS AND SIGNS The Tree Porcupine's feet are specialized for climbing, with long curved claws on each toe. It can climb trees within a couple of days of being born and spends most of its life in trees, so you are very unlikely to see its tracks on the ground. One sign to listen for is the growling sounds it makes; it also sits and shakes its spines to warn off enemies.

COMMENTS This porcupine has a prehensile (gripping) tail to help it climb. There are no spines on the tail, and the upper part is bare of fur and has a rough pad to help the animal hold on tight.

Porcupine Quills

Porcupine quills are a type of hair with a thick covering, and there are about 30,000 on most porcupines. The quills are very sharp and have tiny backward-facing barbs on the end. Once the quill is in the victim's skin, the barbs catch hold and make it very difficult to remove—but they come away from the porcupine easily. The more the victim struggles to get the quill out, the deeper in it goes, and the animal may die if the wound becomes infected.

▶ *Porcupines in some parts of the world destroy trees by eating their bark. This dead tree in India shows signs of having been feasted upon by porcupines.*

Armadillos and Anteaters

Armadillos, anteaters, and pangolins are adapted for feeding on termites and ants. They all have strong claws for breaking open nests and long tongues for lapping up insects. Armadillos and pangolins have armored bodies to protect them from predators and from the bites and stings of their prey. Sloths feed on plants, not insects, and spend their time hanging upside down in trees.

▲ *This Indian Pangolin is sniffing about for termites. If threatened, it tucks its face under its tail and curls into a ball.*

Nine-banded Armadillo

SIZE Body: 18 in (45 cm); tail: 16 in (40 cm)
RANGE Central and southern U.S.A., Mexico, Central and South America
HABITAT Grassland, woodland
FOOD Insects and other small creatures; also eats some fruit and berries
TRACKS AND SIGNS The tracks shows four toes on the front feet and five on the hind feet. The three center toes on the hind feet are much longer than the outer toes. The front track is 1½ in (4 cm) long. You may also see marks of the armadillo's body armor dragging on the ground. Look for signs of feeding activity, such as dug-up earth and anthills. Its droppings are round and contain a lot of dirt.
COMMENTS Listen for these creatures, which grunt as they feed and may not notice you watching if you stand still and stay quiet.

Giant Anteater

SIZE Body: 6½ ft (2 m); tail: 35 in (90 cm)
RANGE Central America, South America
HABITAT Grassland, forest, swamps
FOOD Ants and termites
TRACKS AND SIGNS The Giant Anteater's front feet have four toes, the hind feet, five. The claws on the front feet are so long that the anteater has to walk on its knuckles. Its hind tracks are about 2¾ in (7 cm) wide. Look for damage to termite mounds—a sign that Giant Anteaters may be nearby.
COMMENTS You may notice shallow hollows on the ground where an anteater has scraped out a nest to sleep in.

(H)

◄ SCALE: ½ *life-size*

► LIFE-SIZE *footprint of Giant Anteater*

Northern Tamandua

SIZE Body: 24 in (60 cm); tail: 20 in (50 cm)
RANGE Mexico, Central America, and South America to northern Peru
HABITAT Forest
FOOD Ants and termites; also feeds on other insects, including bees
TRACKS AND SIGNS This anteater is a good climber and spends much of its time in trees. On the ground it leaves tracks with the prints of the long claws on the front feet pointing back or to the side. Like the Giant Anteater, the tamandua has four toes with large claws on its front feet and five on its hind feet. Hind tracks are about 1¾ in (4.5 cm) wide. Look for broken termite nests in trees—usually the work of a tamandua.
COMMENTS This tree-climbing anteater has a prehensile (gripping) tail like some monkeys. It can use this like a fifth limb to hold onto branches as it feeds. The underside of the tail is naked to improve grip.

Slow Sloths

If you catch sight of a sloth you will have no trouble keeping up with it, as these are very slow animals. They can, however, lash out with their long, sharp claws, so make sure not to get too close. There are six species of sloth, all of which live in tropical forests in Central and South America. They are so specialized for life in trees that they cannot walk properly on the ground. The sloth hangs from branches by its hooklike claws, feeding on leaves and other plant material. A pile of droppings by a tree may belong to a sloth. It comes down once a week or so to deposit its droppings.

▲ Sloths spend much of their time motionless and asleep—so much so that green algae often grows on their fur. They are so slow that many predators simply do not notice them.

Kangaroos and Wallabies

Kangaroos and wallabies belong to a group of animals called marsupials and live in Australia and New Guinea. They are plant eaters and often have to travel long distances to find food. Like most marsupials, the female kangaroo has a pouch on the front of her body. A newborn kangaroo makes its way to its mother's pouch, where it can feed on her milk in safety until it has grown big enough to venture out.

▲ The extremely powerful leg muscles of the Red Kangaroo allow it to jump 30 ft (9 m) in one leap.

Red Kangaroo

SIZE Body: 4½ ft (1.4 m); tail: 40 in (1 m)
RANGE Australia (except north and east coasts)
HABITAT Grassland and dry plains
FOOD Grass and other plants
TRACKS AND SIGNS The tracks of a walking kangaroo show pairs of prints—the two small front feet side by side and the two long back feet. The mark of the tail usually appears in the tracks between the hind footprints. When the kangaroo is hopping along on its back feet, you will see a trail showing its hind prints, which are about 10½ in (27 cm) long and quite close together. The hind prints show only two toes, one large, one much smaller, and the pad behind the toes. Look for deep scratches in tree trunks made by male kangaroos as a sign to other males.
COMMENTS This is the largest kangaroo and the largest of all the marsupials.

◄ SCALE: ½ life-size

◄► LIFE-SIZE footprint of Red Kangaroo

Swamp Wallaby

SIZE Body: 34 in (85 cm); tail: 34 in (85 cm)
RANGE Eastern Australia
HABITAT Forest
FOOD A wide variety of leaves and other plant matter
TRACKS AND SIGNS The tracks are similar to, but smaller than, those of the Red Kangaroo. They show imprints of the fourth and fifth toes on the hind feet and five widespread toes on the front feet. You may also see the mark of its tail between the footprints.

COMMENTS
This wallaby is active at night. Despite its name, it does not always live around swamps, but it does always like to have plenty of trees among which to hide.

◀ SCALE: ²/₃ life-size

▶ LIFE-SIZE footprint of Swamp Wallaby

Tree Kangaroo

SIZE Body: 25 in (64 cm); tail: 30 in (75 cm)
RANGE Northeastern Australia
HABITAT Rain forest
FOOD Leaves and fruit
TRACKS AND SIGNS The tracks of this kangaroo show that it has broad back feet up to 6 in (15 cm) long. It can walk and bound in the same ways as the rest of its family, but can also walk by moving its back feet alternately instead of together. It can also move backward, which other kangaroos cannot do.
COMMENTS The Tree Kangaroo is a good climber and can walk or hop along branches. Its front feet are adapted for holding on to branches.

▲ SCALE: ²/₃ life-size

Bounding Kangaroos

Kangaroos have two ways of moving. When feeding, the kangaroo walks slowly on all four legs, using its tail and front feet for support as it moves its hind feet forward, both at the same time. It places its hind feet on either side of its front feet. But when traveling fast, the kangaroo moves in a series of bounds during which the long hind legs act like springs to propel the body forward with some force. The tail helps balance the weight of the front of the body. The Red Kangaroo can cover as much as 30 ft (9 m) in one bound and moves at up to 40 mph (65 km/h).

The Tasmanian Devil, Quolls, and Opossums

Quolls and the Tasmanian Devil belong to the dasyurid or "hairy tail" marsupials. Opossums make up another group and are the only marsupials that live outside Australia, New Zealand, and their neighboring islands. They are rat-shaped, with scaly tails. Members of both groups carry their young either in a pouch or between folds of skin on the belly.

▶ *This scat from a Tasmanian Devil contain the spines of an echidna (see pages 114–115), which the Devil was unable to digest.*

Tasmanian Devil

SIZE Body: 25½ in (65 cm); tail: 10 in (26 cm)
RANGE Tasmania, Australia
HABITAT Forest
FOOD Carrion, such as dead sheep and wallabies; also preys on small mammals, birds, and reptiles
TRACKS AND SIGNS This animal's tracks are squarish and show all toes. The front tracks, at about 2 in (5 cm) wide, are slightly larger than the hind tracks. It usually walks slowly but sometimes bounds, moving its hind feet together. It is most active at night—the best time to spot it is a few hours after sunset. Listen for its loud calls, including coughs and screeches. When anxious, it gives off a foul odor that some say is worse than a skunk's spray—in 2002, it was voted the world's smelliest animal by naturalists.
COMMENTS This is the largest flesh-eating marsupial. Its jaws and teeth are so strong that it can eat nearly every part of its prey, including bones and fur.

Eastern Quoll

SIZE Body: 18 in (45 cm); tail: 12 in (30 cm)
RANGE Southeastern Australia and Tasmania
HABITAT Forest and open country
FOOD Rodents, birds, lizards, insects, other small creatures; also eats fruit, leaves, carrion
TRACKS AND SIGNS This quoll has five toes on the front feet and four on the hind—most quolls have five toes on all four feet. The front print is about 1½ in (4 cm) long. Look for the quoll's burrow, which is often made under a tree stump or rock.
COMMENTS The female gives birth to a large number of young—up to 30. More than half of these die, and the rest stay in the mother's pouch, feeding on her milk, for several weeks.

▲ *This Virginia Opossum is mimicking the appearance of a sick or dead animal, breathing extremely lightly and emitting a foul odor from its anal gland.*

Playing Possum

The Virginia Opossum is well known for its habit of "playing possum"—pretending to be dead if in danger. The animal lies on its side with its eyes shut and its tongue hanging out, in the hope that the predator will lose interest and go away or pay less attention, giving the opossum a chance to escape. Alternatively, the opossum may try a very different tactic and go on the attack—it screeches and hisses at its attacker and bares its 50 teeth to scare it away.

Virginia Opossum

SIZE Body: 20 in (50 cm); tail: 21 in (53 cm)
RANGE United States, Mexico, Central America
HABITAT Forest, farmland, woodland, usually near water
FOOD Insects, birds, frogs, and other small animals; also eats carrion, fruit, and berries
TRACKS AND SIGNS Each foot has five toes, which generally all show in the tracks. The toes of the front feet are widely spread, and the three middle toes are longer than the outer ones. The hind footprints are about 2½ in (6.5 cm) wide and are more unusual. Again the middle three toes are longer, but are side by side, and the outer toes are slanted away from the others. Trails nearly always show paired footprints of the opossum walking, not running.
COMMENTS This animal is the only wild marsupial in North America. Like its Australian relatives, the female has a pouch, where her young live while they grow.

Wombats and Koala

Wombats, the Koala, and bandicoots belong to different marsupial families. There are about 21 kinds of bandicoot (unrelated to Asia's bandicoot rats), all found in Australia and New Guinea. The three wombat species all live in Australia and are bulky, powerful diggers. The Koala lives only in Australia. It is specialized for life in eucalyptus forests and rarely leaves the safety of the trees. All these animals have distinctive tracks.

▲ Wombat scats are cube-shaped and can be found on logs and paths around feeding sites and outside burrows.

Brown Bandicoot

SIZE Body: 14 in (36 cm); tail: 5½ in (14 cm)
RANGE Southeastern Australia, Southwestern Australia, Queensland, Tasmania
HABITAT Woodland and thick scrub
FOOD Insects, worms, lizards, berries
TRACKS AND SIGNS Bandicoot trails show long footprints. Only three of its five toes show in the front tracks and sometimes two in the hind tracks. The front track is 1¼ in (3 cm) long; the hind track is about twice as long. The bandicoot moves its front legs alternately and its hind legs together, but it does not hop on its hind legs like kangaroos do.
COMMENTS Bandicoots use their strong, clawed front feet to dig holes and then root around with their long snouts to find insects and larvae to eat. Look for small holes about the size of a bandicoot's snout.

Common Wombat

SIZE Body: 4 ft (1.2 m); tail: 1¼ in (3 cm)
RANGE Eastern Australia, Tasmania
HABITAT Forest and scrub
FOOD Grass, roots, plant stems, fungi
TRACKS AND SIGNS The Common Wombat's large, flat-footed tracks are quite easy to recognize. It has five toes on each foot, and it usually leaves clear claw marks with its large claws, particularly in the front tracks, which are 2½ in (6.5 cm) long. Look for V-shaped marks where the wombat has clawed the ground after leaving its droppings.
COMMENTS The wombat likes to have dust-baths in soft earth, lying on its side and throwing dust over its body. A common sign is pathways leading from the burrow to feeding areas.

Koala

SIZE Body: 32 in (80 cm); tail: none
RANGE Eastern Australia
HABITAT Eucalyptus forest and woodland
FOOD Eucalyptus leaves and shoots
TRACKS AND SIGNS The Koala spends much of its time in trees, but its tracks are sometimes seen beneath its feeding trees. Its footprints are up to 6 in (15 cm) long, and on the front foot, the first and second toes point away from the rest of the foot. The large, curved claws also leave marks. Look for scratches in tree trunks left by the Koala as it climbs and for droppings under their feeding trees.

Droppings contain bits of leaf and may smell of eucalyptus.
COMMENTS The Koala's front feet are adapted for holding its food—the first toes can be held against the other three to help the animal grip.

Wombat Burrows

All three wombat species use their long claws to dig vast burrows in which to shelter during the day. The burrow may stretch many yards and be up to 6 ft (2 m) deep. The animal digs with its front feet and kicks the soil out of the way with its back feet. Any plant roots in the way are quickly disposed of with the wombat's strong teeth. The entrance is quite large to admit the bulky wombat and often oval in shape. A wombat may have three or more burrows, and several wombats may use the same burrow.

▶ *A Common Wombat young clings to its mother's back in a burrow. Wombats can be very aggressive if disturbed.*

Egg-laying Mammals

The echidnas and Platypus are the only animals in a group of mammals called monotremes. These animals all lay eggs instead of giving birth to live young. However, they do have body hair, and they feed their young on milk like other mammals do. Both the Long- and Short-nosed Echidnas are covered in coarse hairs and spines. The Platypus has a beaklike mouth and webbed feet and spends much of its life in water.

◀ *Short-nosed Echidnas may be found in many environments in Australia, including urban parkland.*

Long-nosed Echidna

SIZE Body: 32 in (80 cm); tail: 2 in (5 cm)
RANGE New Guinea
HABITAT Forest
FOOD Earthworms and other soil-living creatures
TRACKS AND SIGNS The tracks of these creatures are rare. It has five toes on each foot, and the three middle ones usually have sharp claws for digging. The male has a spur on each back leg.
COMMENTS Instead of teeth, this animal has small hooked spines on its tongue, which help it gather earthworms to eat.

Short-nosed Echidna

SIZE Body: 14 in (36 cm); tail: 4 in (10 cm)

RANGE Australia, Tasmania, New Guinea
HABITAT Grassland, forest, plains, rocky areas
FOOD Ants and termites
TRACKS AND SIGNS The front footprints, which turn slightly inward, are 1½ in (4 cm) long and show all five toes and strong claws. The hind prints show four claws, two of them very long. These long claws help the echidna groom itself. Look out for damaged ant and termite nests and rotting logs that have been torn apart by echidnas searching for food.
COMMENTS Short-nosed Echidnas shelter in hollow logs, among rocks, or in burrows abandoned by other animals. They will dig themselves into the soil if in danger.

Platypus

SIZE Body: 16 in (40 cm); tail: 6 in (15 cm)
RANGE Eastern Australia, Tasmania
HABITAT Lakes and rivers in wooded areas
FOOD Shellfish, larvae, frogs, fish
TRACKS AND SIGNS The Platypus is a strong swimmer with webbed feet, but its tracks are sometimes seen on muddy riverbanks. When it walks on land, the webbing is folded back so its claw marks show in its tracks. The webbing on the hind feet, which are 2 in (5 cm) long, stops farther back before the toes. The tail drags on the ground and shows in trails.
COMMENTS The male Platypus has a spur on each ankle that connects to poison glands in the thighs. The spurs are used against predators or rival males but not to kill prey.

Platypus Burrows

The Platypus digs short burrows in the riverbank above the water level for shelter. But in the breeding season, the female digs a longer burrow and lays her eggs in a chamber at the end, on a nest of dry grass and leaves. She stays with her eggs most of the time to keep them warm, leaving only briefly to feed. When the young hatch, they are tiny, blind, and helpless, and they stay in the burrow for several months. Look out for burrow entrances, which often show an area of flattened mud leading down to the water.

▼ *This Platypus is diving in search of freshwater crayfish, which it digs out of the riverbed using its snout. It carries them to the surface in its cheek pouches.*

Amphibians and Reptiles

Like mammals and birds, amphibians and reptiles are vertebrates—they have a backbone. Amphibians include frogs, toads, newts, and salamanders, which live both on land and in water. The main reptile groups are turtles, snakes, lizards, and crocodiles. Lightweight creatures, such as frogs and lizards, rarely leave tracks, but you can find tracks of heavier reptiles such as tortoises and alligators. Ocean-living turtles leave tracks in the sand when they come up onto beaches to lay their eggs. Snakes may also leave tracks, particularly on sand. Other signs to look for are the shed skins of snakes and lizards and jellylike masses of frog and toad eggs in ponds.

◄ *The Australian Woma Python hunts small mammals, lizards, and ground birds. It catches many creatures in burrows, where it has no room to wrap its victim in coils. Instead, it pushes against the prey to crush it. Woma Pythons often bear the scars of rodents that put up a fight.*

Frogs, Toads, and Newts

Frogs and toads are amphibians, which means they can live both on land and in water. They have long back legs, webbed toes, and no tail. Their skin is often moist. Most feed on small creatures such as insects, slugs, and snails, which they catch with their long, sticky tongue. Newts and salamanders are amphibians with a long body and tail. Like frogs and toads, most newts and salamanders lay their eggs in water.

◀ *You may spot frogs sitting on water lily leaves floating on the water surface. They generally stay near water.*

American Toad

SIZE Body: 4 in (11 cm); tail: none
RANGE Eastern North America
HABITAT Varied, including forests and backyards
FOOD Insects are its main food, but also eats spiders, snails, and worms
TRACKS AND SIGNS The tracks of toads are not often seen, but you may spot some on a muddy riverbank. Footprints show four toes on the front feet and the five webbed toes on each hind foot. Hind tracks are up to 1¼ in (3 cm) long, the front tracks about ¾ in (2 cm).
COMMENTS This toad is usually active at night and hides in a burrow or under a stone or a log during the day.

Bullfrog

SIZE Body: 8 in (20 cm); tail: none
RANGE North America; introduced in parts of Europe
HABITAT Lakes, ponds, streams
FOOD Insects, fish, smaller frogs; sometimes birds and snakes
TRACKS AND SIGNS Tracks of frogs are rarely seen, but this large frog spends more time than some on land, and its trails may be seen on muddy banks. Like the toad, the Bullfrog has five toes on each hind foot, four on each front foot. Its feet are narrower than those of the toad. The front tracks are about ¾ in (2 cm) long, the hind tracks are up to 1¼ in (3 cm) long.
COMMENTS The Bullfrog is the largest frog in North America. Listen for its loud, deep-voiced call.

▲ The dark specks in this mass of frogspawn are eggs covered in protective jelly. Most frogs and toads lay their eggs in ponds and streams; some use a moist place in a tree or on the ground.

Eastern Newt

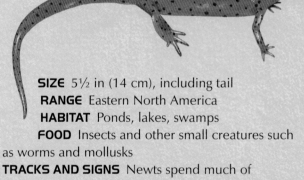

SIZE 5½ in (14 cm), including tail

RANGE Eastern North America

HABITAT Ponds, lakes, swamps

FOOD Insects and other small creatures such as worms and mollusks

TRACKS AND SIGNS Newts spend much of their time in water, but their tracks may sometimes be found on the sides of muddy ponds. The tracks are about ¼ in (5 mm) long. They show four toes on the front feet and five on the hind. A thick line made by the newt's belly or tail often appears between the footprints.

COMMENTS Look carefully in shallow water, and you may see this fierce little hunter searching for prey.

Ⓗ

From Egg to Adult

Frogs and toads reproduce by laying eggs in a mass of jellylike clumps stuck together. The eggs hatch into little swimming creatures called tadpoles, which have a tail and feathery gills for breathing in water. As a tadpole grows, it develops legs and lungs. It becomes a miniature version of the adult and loses its tail and gills. Now it is able to spend at least some of its life on land. Look for a mass of eggs, or frogspawn, in shallow ponds, but do not disturb it. Each tiny clump in the spawn contains a dark egg. Toads lay their eggs in long threads.

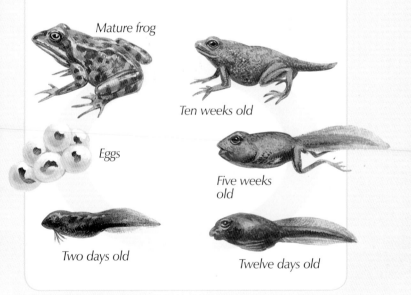

Mature frog

Ten weeks old

Eggs

Five weeks old

Two days old

Twelve days old

Crocodiles, Caimans, and Alligators

The crocodile family includes caimans, alligators, and the Gharial, as well as crocodiles. These large reptiles live in tropical and subtropical areas and can move in water and on land. They have short legs and a long body covered with hard scales and thickened bony plates. Their long jaws are studded with sharp teeth for catching their prey. Track crocodiles or alligators only in the company of a very experienced guide.

▲ *To avoid overheating, crocodiles gape—they lie still with their jaws open to lose heat through their mouths.*

Nile Crocodile

SIZE Up to 20 ft (6 m) long
RANGE Africa south of the Sahara
HABITAT Lakes, swamps, large rivers
FOOD Young crocodiles feed mostly on insects, then move on to fish, frogs, and small mammals; adults attack large mammals such as antelope and zebra, often at water holes
TRACKS AND SIGNS The tracks of these heavy animals may be seen on muddy banks. A crocodile has five toes on the front feet and four on the hind feet, which are webbed. Hind feet tracks are up to 10 in (25 cm) long, much larger than the front tracks, which are up to about 4¼ in (11 cm) long.

You may also see marks of the large tail dragging on the ground.
COMMENTS Crocodiles have V-shaped snouts, but alligators have broader, U-shaped snouts. When an alligator's mouth is closed, you can see only its upper teeth, but in crocodiles you can also see the large fourth tooth jutting out from the lower jaw. Crocodiles lie in wait for their prey, almost totally submerged in the water. Look for their eyes and nostrils above the water surface. Never go near water in places where there could be crocodiles.

Spectacled Caiman

SIZE Length: 8½ ft (2.6 m)
RANGE Central and South America; introduced in Florida

HABITAT Lakes, ponds, swamps
FOOD Crabs, snails, fish
TRACKS AND SIGNS Look out for marks of the caiman sliding into the water from the riverbank. If you see the wide imprint of the body with tracks on either side, stay well away from that stretch of water.
COMMENTS This caiman gets its name from the ridge on the head between the eyes, which looks like the bridge of a pair of eyeglasses.

American Alligator

◄ SCALE: ⅕ *life-size*

SIZE Up to 15 ft (4.5 m) long
RANGE Southeastern U.S.A.
HABITAT Lakes, rivers, ponds, swamps
FOOD Fish, snakes, turtles, birds, and mammals such as raccoons and the Nutria
TRACKS AND SIGNS Like crocodiles and caimans, the American Alligator has five toes on the front feet and four on the hind. The hind feet are partly webbed. The front track is about 4 in (10 cm) long, the hind about 8 in (20 cm) long. Alligators are noisy animals, so listen for the bellowing roars of adults and the higher-pitched calls of young.
COMMENTS Like crocodiles, alligators mate in water and lay their eggs on land. The female makes a mound of earth and plants to keep her eggs warm. She guards the eggs until they are ready to hatch and opens up the mound when she hears her young calling to her. Look for signs of nest mounds or eggshells in alligator areas in late summer.

Caring Mom

Crocodile females are devoted parents. A mother lies near her eggs and keeps guard while they are incubating. Once her babies hatch, she picks them up in her mouth and carries them to a safe stretch of water. She continues to guard them fiercely until they are large enough to fend for themselves.

► *A mother crocodile guards her eggs until they hatch.*

Snakes

Snakes are reptiles that range in size from a few inches to more than 30 ft (9 m). Most are carnivorous. They travel using wavelike movements. Pointed scales on their belly help them grip and move over surfaces. They have a long, forked tongue and no legs, ear openings, or moveable eyelids. Some, such as boas, suffocate their prey using their strong body coils. Others, such as vipers and Australia's tiger snakes, have a poisonous bite. Tiger snakes are among the most deadly snakes in the world.

◀ *In summer, European Grass Snakes lay their eggs in warm spots, such as compost heaps or beneath rotting logs.*

Boa Constrictor

SIZE Up to 18 ft (5.5 m) long—most are smaller
RANGE Northern Mexico to Argentina
HABITAT Deserts, rain forest, grassland, farmland
FOOD Lizards, birds, small mammals such as opossums, rats, and squirrels; also preys on bats, which it catches while hanging from a tree branch and seizing the bat as it flies by
TRACKS AND SIGNS Boa Constrictors shed their skin every couple of months. The great length of the sloughed skin may help in identification. Look for trails on muddy river margins. Boas often use concertina locomotion when hunting, but will use serpentine movement when trying to escape in a hurry.
COMMENTS This is one of the largest snakes in the Americas. It kills by constriction—it wraps its coils around its prey not to crush it but to stop it breathing. The prey dies from suffocation.

Sidewinder

SIZE Up to 32 in (82 cm) long
RANGE Southwestern U.S.A. and Mexico
HABITAT Desert and scrub
FOOD Rats, mice
TRACKS AND SIGNS This snake leaves a distinctive trail of J-shaped markings, which may be seen on sandy ground. Sidewinding is the most efficient form of movement for a snake on sandy surfaces.
COMMENTS The Sidewinder is a rattlesnake, so it has a rattle on the end of its tail, with which it makes a rattling sound to warn enemies to keep their distance. The rattle is actually made up of the tips of the tail left behind each time the snake sheds its skin. The Sidewinder tracks down its prey with the help of heat-sensitive pits on its head. It kills by biting the prey with its long curved fangs and injecting venom.

Snake Movement

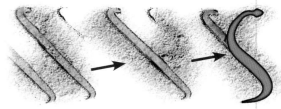

Serpentine

movement (weaving from side-to-side) is the most common way for snakes to move. By pressing against any tiny lump or bump on the ground, the snake is able to push itself forward, leaving behind a characteristic trail in sand or mud.

Sidewinding

is used by snakes that need to move on loose sand. The snake throws its body forward in sideways-moving waves, with only two short sections touching the ground. It leaves a trail of parallel, J-shaped markings.

Concertina movement

is often used by large snakes such as the Boa Constrictor. The snake uses its belly scales to anchor itself against a rough surface and inches forward with a rippling muscular movement. All snakes can use this type of movement, but most use it only for climbing trees or moving through tunnels, so trails are rare.

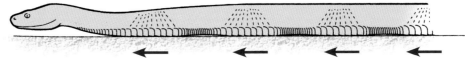

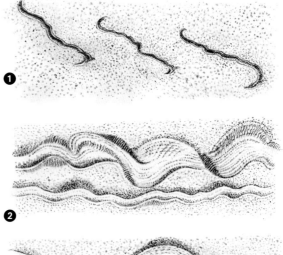

European Grass Snake

SIZE Up to 4 ft (1.2 m) long
RANGE Europe, northwestern Africa, central Asia
HABITAT Damp meadows, marshes, ditches
FOOD Frogs, toads, newts, fish; also sometimes eats birds and small mammals
TRACKS AND SIGNS Grass Snakes lay their eggs in piles of vegetation—often in warm compost heaps—and you may see signs of the shells once the young have hatched. If you do come across unhatched eggs, do not touch or disturb them. You may also see trails on muddy riverbanks.
COMMENTS The Grass Snake swims well and spends some of its time in water hunting prey. This snake swallows much of its prey alive; although it secretes a venom that is poisonous to small animals, its bite is not harmful to humans.

Which type of movement made which track?

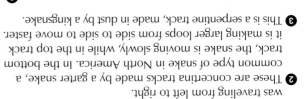

❶

❷

❸

❸ This is a serpentine track, made in dust by a kingsnake.

❷ These are concertina tracks made by a garter snake, a common type of snake in North America. In the bottom track, the snake is moving slowly, while in the top track it is making larger loops from side to side to move faster.

❶ This is a sidewinder track made in sand. The rattlesnake was traveling from left to right.

Snake and Lizard Skins

Many people think that snakes are slimy to the touch, but they are not. A snake feels dry and smooth. Its body is covered with lots of tiny scales made of keratin—the same material your fingernails are made of. These scales are just the top layer of skin. Underneath is a thicker layer, and this contains the pigment cells that give a snake's skin its different colors.

Shedding skin

A snake's skin does not grow with its body, as ours does. Every so often, the snake has to shed its outer layer of skin because it has become too small for its body. A snake may shed its skin up to seven times in its first year, but it will molt less often as it gets older. To shed its skin, the snake starts to rub its head on the ground or against a tree or other hard surface. It rubs until the skin breaks and starts to peel back. Then the snake slowly crawls out of its skin, which turns inside out in the process like a dirty sock. The new layer of skin has already grown beneath the old layer, so the snake is never without its outer layer of protection.

▲ *The shed skin of a Gaboon Viper hangs from a branch. The skin is turned completely inside out.*

▼ *This Dione Rat Snake emerges headfirst from its old skin, which has become too small. Any external parasites living on the snake will be left behind with the skin.*

◄ *A Gaboon Viper lies patiently in wait for unsuspecting prey. It is superbly camouflaged to blend in with the leaf litter scattered on the rain forest floor.*

Skin colors

Many snakes are colored to blend with their background. The long, thin green Vine Snake, for example, is bright green like the creepers and vines it lives among in Central and South America. And the Gaboon Viper has ornate brownish patterns on its skin, which make it very difficult to see as it lies among fallen, dying leaves.

Other snakes are very brightly colored. Their bold markings may serve as a warning to potential predators to stay away from their poisonous fangs. The many species of coral snake, for example, have bright red, black, and yellow bands ringing the body. There are a couple of harmless snakes that look very much the same—the Scarlet Snake and the Scarlet Kingsnake. They probably gain protection from predators by mimicking their poisonous relatives. Beware—if you see any of these brightly colored snakes, always assume that they are venomous and stay away.

Lizards

Lizards need to shed their skin regularly, too, but it does not come off all in one piece. A lizard sheds its skin a bit at a time. It may rub itself against stones or other objects to help remove skin. It may also tear off pieces with its mouth and eat them.

▶ *This Cardamom Forest Gecko from Southeast Asia is rubbing itself against tree bark to help it shed its old skin.*

Lizards

▲ The giant Komodo Dragon of Indonesia uses its long tongue to smell the air. It can detect carrion from several miles away.

Lizards are the largest group of reptiles. There are at least 3,500 different species and they live in most parts of the world, except the coldest areas. The tiniest are the geckos, at only 3 in (7.5 cm) long; the largest is the huge Komodo Dragon, which can be up to 10 ft (3 m) long. Most lizards have a long body and tail and four legs, but there are legless species, too. Lizards generally live on the ground and in trees. Most are too small and light to leave tracks, except on very soft ground, but you may see them scurrying around as they search for food.

Nile Monitor Lizard

SIZE Up to 6½ ft (2 m) long
RANGE Non-desert regions throughout Africa, except northwest
HABITAT Always near water such as rivers and lakes.
FOOD Frogs, fish, shellfish such as crabs and mussels, birds and their eggs
TRACKS AND SIGNS This large lizard often leaves tracks, showing five toes on both front and hind feet. The tracks of the front feet are about 2¼ in (6 cm) long, but the hind prints are up to 4¼ in (11 cm). You may also see the mark of its stout tail dragging on the ground.
COMMENTS The Nile Monitor is a strong swimmer and uses its broad tail as a rudder. It also climbs trees with the help of its large claws and strong tail.

Brook's Gecko

SIZE Up to 6 in (15 cm)
RANGE Asia, Africa, South America, West Indies
HABITAT Varied, including forest and grassland
FOOD Insects
TRACKS AND SIGNS Trails of these little creatures are rare, as with all but large lizards. If a track is made, it is easily identified by the small disks at the end of each toe, which this gecko species, like many others, uses to grip and walk on smooth vertical surfaces. The hind tracks are about ½ in (1.5 cm); the front tracks are slightly smaller. Listen for this lizard's loud call, too, which sounds like "gekoh" and is the reason for its common name.
COMMENTS If grabbed by a predator, geckos can shed their tails easily to help them escape; the muscles contract quickly to prevent blood loss, and a new tail grows in a few weeks.

Frilled Lizard

SIZE Body: 12 in (30 cm);
tail: 24 in (60 cm)
RANGE Northern Australia, New Guinea
HABITAT Dry forest, grassy woodland
FOOD Ants, termites, other insects, spiders, small lizards and mammals
TRACKS AND SIGNS This lizard stays up in trees nearly all the time and lives in grassy areas, so tracks are rarely seen; you may spot it on low branches. In spring and summer you may find its open nest dug about 4 in (10 cm) into sandy soil, with a clutch of 8–15 soft-shelled small white eggs. The eggs are tiny—only about ½ in (1 cm) long.
COMMENTS If you get close to a Frilled Lizard, you may be lucky enough to see its startling display. If threatened, the lizard opens its mouth wide and hisses, unfurling a brightly colored ruff of skin up to 20 in (30 cm) wide around its neck to make itself look bigger. It may then run away on its hind legs.

Speedy Climbers

Geckos can scamper up the smoothest walls and walk upside down on ceilings with the greatest ease. They can do this because of a little disklike pad at the end of each toe. The pads on a single foot are covered in millions of tiny bristles tipped with suction cups, which help the feet hold fast to almost any surface.

▼ *The tuatara lives in colder climates than most reptiles. It is active at temperatures as low as 45°F (7°C), and those above 82°F (28°C) can kill it. It is active mainly at night.*

Tuatara

There are just two kinds of tuatara, both living on islands off New Zealand. The tuatara looks like a lizard but is actually in a group all of its own. It is like related reptiles that lived more than 130 million years ago. Tuataras shelter in burrows and feed on small creatures such as crickets, worms, snails, and lizards.

Turtles and Tortoises

There are about 230 different species of turtles and tortoises. Some live on land, others in fresh water, and a few very large turtles live in the sea. Most have a hard shell made of horn and bone to protect the soft body. The shell is in two parts, the upper shell (the carapace) and the lower (the plastron). Most turtles and tortoises can pull their head under the shell for protection. They have no teeth. Instead, they have hard beaks.

▲ *A hatchling Leatherback Turtle makes its way across the beach to the sea, leaving a trail of V-shaped tracks in the sand.*

Spur-thighed Tortoise

SIZE 6 in (15 cm) long
RANGE North Africa, southern Europe, Middle East
HABITAT Woodland, cultivated land, meadows
FOOD Mainly plants and some insects and other small creatures such as snails; also carnivore droppings to obtain calcium, which, like all tortoises and turtles, they need to keep their bones and shells in good condition
TRACKS AND SIGNS The tracks of this species show five very broad, rounded claws on the front feet and four on the hind feet. The tracks are about 1¼ in (3 cm) wide. Look for small, pointed droppings, too, which contain mainly plant matter.
COMMENTS If it feels threatened or scared, the Spur-thighed Tortoise, like most other tortoises, can pull its head and legs into its shell for protection.

Common Snapping Turtle

SIZE Shell: up to 20 in (50 cm); tail: up to 15 in (40 cm)
RANGE Eastern North America, Mexico, Central America
HABITAT Marshes, ponds, rivers, lakes
FOOD All kinds of water and bankside life, including fish, amphibians, mammals, birds, and plants
TRACKS AND SIGNS This turtle spends much of its time in water, but you may see its tracks, which are 2 in (5 cm) wide, on muddy banks. The long tail may leave a line between the footprints.
COMMENTS An excellent swimmer, the Common Snapping Turtle also likes to wait for its prey at the river bottom, hidden by aquatic plants. In the cooler areas of their range, Common Snapping Turtles hibernate in winter.

Leatherback Turtle

SIZE Up to 6½ ft (2 m)

RANGE Warm areas of all the world's oceans

HABITAT Deep open ocean

FOOD Mainly jellyfish

TRACKS AND SIGNS Males never leave the sea. The female does so only to nest, choosing a moonless night so that predators do not see her, and laying eggs several times a month from May to July. The nests are hidden beneath the sand above the high-tide line. After 60–70 days the hatchlings make their way to the sea after dark, leaving a trail of V-shaped tracks (*see* opposite).

COMMENTS This is the world's largest turtle and can weigh as much as 1,600 lb (727 kg).

Nesting Turtles

Sea turtles live in the sea and come to land only to lay eggs. Every couple of years, the turtles travel to their breeding area and mate. The female then drags herself up onto the beach, uses her flippers to dig a pit, lays her eggs, and covers them with sand. When the young hatch, they must make their own way to the sea. Many are caught by birds and other predators.

▲ *Freshwater turtles make their nests in sandy soil near water. The broken eggshells around the entrance to this nest show it has been raided, perhaps by a fox or a raccoon.*

Birds

A bird is a vertebrate animal with a strong but light body, two legs, and a pair of wings. All birds are covered with feathers, which keep them warm and streamline the body. Most, but not all, birds can fly. Birds are generally easier to spot than mammals but many spend little time on the ground so their tracks are not often seen. Listen for their calls and look for molted feathers, which are one of the most commonly found animal signs. Be on the watch for feeding signs, such as beak marks on fir cones, broken nut shells, and holes in tree trunks. Look, too, for birds' nests—but never touch any eggs you see.

◄ *The Bald Eagle prefers to live near lakes, rivers, or coasts where it can catch its favorite food—fish. It not only catches its own prey but also scavenges dead animals. It also chases other birds and even attacks them to make them drop their catches, which it then steals.*

▲ *The bulky, cup-shaped magpie nest may be spotted in woods or sometimes buildings. Never touch eggs in nests.*

Crows

Crows and their relatives—the rooks, ravens, magpies, and jays—are intelligent birds. They are very adaptable, will eat almost anything, and often develop clever new ways to find food or steal from other birds. Many can kill prey as large as rabbits. They also feed on carrion—animals that are already dead. Most crows are large birds with a powerful beak. Their legs are strong, so they can move fast on the ground as well as in the air. Crows are not shy birds and you will often see them in cities, as well as in country areas.

American Crow

SIZE Body and tail: up to 21 in (53 cm); wingspan: 3¼ ft (1 m)

RANGE North America

HABITAT Woodland, farmland, orchards, parks, suburban areas

FOOD Insects, spiders, frogs, lizards, small mammals, birds and their eggs, grain, fruit, nuts

TRACKS AND SIGNS These common birds are easy to spot. You may hear their harsh "caw-caw" call. Their large, untidy nests are made on trees, bushes, or even telegraph poles. Crows spend much time walking on the ground with long strides, so you may see clear tracks on mud or snow. The tracks, about 2 in (5 cm) long, show three toes pointing forward and one backward. Crows sometimes bounce along, leaving pairs of prints.

COMMENTS Crows are among the birds that have adapted best to life in towns and cities. They scavenge in trash cans and explore backyards and farmland in search of food.

Black-billed Magpie

SIZE Body and tail: up to 20 in (50 cm); wingspan: 24 in (61 cm)

RANGE Western North America, Europe, Asia

HABITAT Open woodland

FOOD Insects, snails, slugs, spiders; also eats small mammals, grain, and carrion, as well as fruit and nuts

TRACKS AND SIGNS Look for this bird's black and white feathers and its long tail, which is black with blue-and-green. It makes a large domed nest of sticks and twigs in a bush or tree. Its tracks are very similar to those of the crow but slightly smaller. Claw marks usually show on all four toes.

COMMENTS Magpies are well known for their thieving habits. They take eggs and young from other birds' nests and are attracted to bright, shiny objects, such as bottle tops and jewelry, which they take to their own nests.

▲ *Crows will eat almost anything, including dead animals. This crow is feeding on a dead rabbit. You might spot signs of a crow's meal, such as clumps of fur or feathers.*

Eggs of the Crow Family

Crows usually lay 3–6 eggs, about 1½ in (4 cm) long. The eggs are green to blue-green in color and speckled with darker brown and gray markings. Magpies lay 5–8 eggs, about 1¼ in (3.5 cm) long, which are pale blue or greenish-blue with spots and speckles and a smooth, glossy surface. Jays lay 5–7 glossy pale green, olive green, or buff-colored speckled eggs, 1¼ in (3.5 cm) long. Never touch or disturb any eggs that you see.

Eurasian Jay

SIZE Body and tail: up to 13 in (34 cm); wingspan: 24 in (60 cm)
RANGE Europe, North Africa, Asia
HABITAT Woodland, farmland, parks, urban areas
FOOD Insects and other small creatures, acorns, berries, grain
TRACKS AND SIGNS Jays are more shy than many of their relatives. Look for a flash of white or blue plumage as a jay flies from tree to tree, and listen for its loud screaming call. Acorns are a favorite food, so you often see jays around oak trees. The nest is made of twigs in a tree and lined with grass and animal hair. Like those of other members of the crow family, the tracks tend to turn slightly inward. They are similar in shape but slightly smaller than those of the crow.
COMMENTS Look out for jays burying supplies of acorns in the fall for use during the winter months.

Feathers

Birds are the only animals that have feathers. All birds, even those that cannot fly, are covered with feathers, which are made of keratin, the same material that our hair and nails are made from. You often find bird feathers on the ground, but it is not always easy to figure out what type of bird they came from unless you have other signs.

What are feathers for?

Feathers provide warmth and are windproof and waterproof. For many kinds of bird, the color of its feathers helps it hide from enemies or attract mates. But, most importantly, the large, strong feathers on a bird's wings and tail allow it to fly. Birds have different types of feathers.

◄ *A Bald Eagle uses its long white tail feathers to steer while it flies.*

Small feathers cover most of the body and keep it warm and streamlined. Underneath these are light, fluffy feathers called down feathers, which add warmth. Water birds, such as ducks and geese, have lots of down feathers. The largest, strongest feathers are on the wings and these are called flight feathers. At the front of the wing are primary flight feathers, and behind these are secondary flight feathers. Many birds also have long, and sometimes very decorative, tail feathers.

◄ *These tracks clearly show the wing prints of a bird taking off, together with those of a mammal—possibly a predator that scared the bird.*

How is a feather made?

A typical feather has a central stem called the quill. A series of branches, called barbs, grow out from each side of the quill. Usually there are lots of small side branches, called barbules, on the barbs, and these mesh with each other, like the teeth of a zipper, to make the body of the feather. Each feather grows from a tiny hole, called a follicle, in a bird's skin.

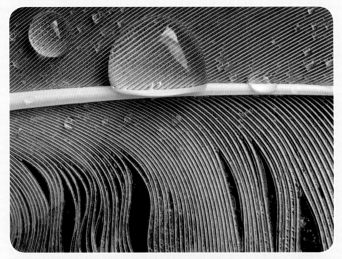

▲ *The barbs that grow out from a feather's central quill are held together by tiny barbules, making the feather waterproof.*

Types of Feathers

Here are pictures of the main types of feathers: body feathers, filoplumes, flight feathers, down feathers, tail feathers, and wing feathers. The flight feathers are usually the largest, but some birds, such as pheasants and peacocks, have very long tail feathers to help them attract mates.

Body, or contour, feathers cover the bird's head and body and keep it streamlined for flight.

Down feathers are the smallest, softest feathers. They provide extra warmth.

Filoplumes are simple, stiff feathers that lie beneath the body feathers. They have very few barbs, or even none at all. Scientists have yet to determine the function of these feathers.

Tail feathers are long and decorative in some cases, but in others they help a bird steer and keep its balance while in the air.

Primary flight feathers are at the outer edge of the wing. Most birds have 10 or 11 primary feathers on each wing.

Secondary wing feathers are on the inside of the wing. Birds have between 9 and 40 secondary feathers on each wing.

Finding feathers

Feathers become damaged and have to be replaced regularly, so birds must molt (lose their feathers) and grow new ones. You may find feathers that have been molted or lost through injury or attack by a mammal or another bird. When a predator such as a hawk or a fox kills a bird, it may eat some of the feathers, but plenty will be left behind. Large feathers, such as those from the wings or tail, are generally the easiest to identify. If you find a feather, you can use the pictures above to try to work out which part of the bird it came from.

Pheasants, Grouse, and Chickens

Pheasants, chickens, and their relatives are known as game birds because most kinds, such as grouse, have long been hunted. Most of these birds have a sturdy, rounded body and short, strong legs. Some, such as pheasants, have colorful feathers. Game birds spend much of their time on the ground, but they can fly and often roost in trees. You can spot their tracks on muddy ground or in snow.

▲ *A clutch of pale brown Black Grouse eggs lies in a shallow nest lined with leaves, twigs, and grass.*

Ring-necked Pheasant

SIZE Body and tail: up to 28 in (70 cm); wingspan: 34 in (86 cm)
RANGE Asia; introduced in Europe, North America, New Zealand, many other parts of the world
HABITAT Open country, woodland, woodland edges
FOOD Seeds, grains, plant shoots, invertebrates, other small animals
TRACKS AND SIGNS You may spot this bird scurrying out of a hedgerow or find one of its long, coppery feathers with dark markings. The nest is a hollow in the ground lined with plants or grass. You may spot piles of brownish-black droppings on the ground near nests or roosting sites—these are firm in winter, more liquid in summer. Its tracks show three widely spread, forward-pointing toes tipped with sturdy claws. The back toe is smaller and usually only the claw shows in tracks, which are about 3 in (7.5 cm) long.
COMMENTS The male is larger than the female and has beautiful dark green and coppery markings. The female has plainer, brownish plumage.

Game Bird Eggs

The Ring-necked Pheasant lays 7–15 eggs, which are a smooth olive-brown color, and about 1¾ in (4.5 cm) long. The prairie chicken, both Lesser and Greater species, lays 12–14 eggs, which may be light to deep browny beige, sometimes speckled with brown. They are about 1¾ in (4.5 cm) long. The eggs of the Red-legged Partridge have a glossy surface and are brownish-yellow, spotted with darker markings. A clutch contains 10–16 eggs about 1½ in (4 cm) long.

▲ *Willow Ptarmigans usually feed on coarse plants. Their droppings, shown above, are tube-shaped pellets about ¾ in (2 cm) long that contain stems and seeds.*

Red-legged Partridge

SIZE Body and tail: up to 13 in (34 cm)
RANGE Europe; introduced in U.S.A.
HABITAT Scrub, moorland, farmland
FOOD Seeds, roots, insects
TRACKS AND SIGNS You may spot these birds, also known as Chukars, feeding on the ground. They can fly but prefer to escape from danger by running. The nest is a shallow hollow on the ground lined with leaves. Listen for the male's deep call, which sounds like "chuck-chuck-chuff." The tracks are similar to the pheasant's but only about 2 in (5 cm) long. You can see them most often in snow.
COMMENTS Male and female partridges look alike. Look for the white throat patch, striped flanks, and red beak and legs.

Greater Prairie Chicken ▲

SIZE Body and tail: up to 17 in (43 cm); wingspan: 28 in (71 cm)
RANGE North America: northwest Texas and neighboring states
HABITAT Prairie grassland
FOOD Plant matter such as leaves, fruit, and grain; also eats insects, particularly in summer
TRACKS AND SIGNS Listen for the male bird's booming and whooping calls. The nest is a shallow scrape in the ground, often under overhanging plants. Prairie chicken tracks, in both the Lesser and Greater species, are shorter than those of pheasants, at about 2½ in (6 cm) long, and the fourth, backward-pointing toe may show. The tracks are most often seen in snow.
COMMENTS Male prairie chickens gather in groups to perform spectacular courtship displays in the breeding season.

Ducks and Geese

▲ *These eggs were laid by a Canada Goose. Both parents will protect the nest while the eggs incubate.*

Ducks, geese, and swans usually live in and around water. Most have strong legs and webbed feet and are good swimmers. They find much of their food in water, and some even dive beneath the surface. Beaks vary according to feeding methods but are usually broad and flattened. These birds generally nest on the ground, and their young are able to walk about and even swim only hours after hatching. Most of this group are large birds, and their webbed feet often leave clear tracks on riverbanks and soft ground.

Tundra Swan

SIZE Body and tail: up to 4½ ft (1.4 m); wingspan: 6½ ft (1.7 m)

RANGE North America, northern Europe, Asia

HABITAT Tundra lakes and ponds, marshland, estuaries

FOOD Water plants, seeds, grains; also small creatures such as snails and clams

TRACKS AND SIGNS You are most likely to see this swan on water. Listen for its loud honking calls. The nest is a mound of plants and moss made near water, with a hollow in the middle for eggs. You may see greenish, cylindrical droppings on the shore near nesting sites. Swans are heavy birds so usually leave clear tracks that show webbing, toes, and claws. The tracks are similar to goose tracks but larger, up to about 7 in (18 cm) long.

COMMENTS These large birds can be surprisingly fierce, especially if they have young, so do not get too close.

▶ SCALE: ¹/₅ life-size

Waterfowl Eggs

The Mallard usually lays 10–12 pale green eggs, which are about 2¼ in (5.5 cm) long. The female Mallard incubates the eggs alone and her young are able to run around and swim soon after hatching. The Canada Goose lays 2–8 eggs, which are creamy white in color and about 3¼ in (8.5 cm) long. The Tundra Swan usually lays about 5 large, creamy white eggs, which are up to 4 in (10 cm) long.

◀ LIFE-SIZE *footprint of Tundra Swan*

▲ *If you spot Snow Geese in flight, you will often see them in a V-formation. They fly like this to reduce wind drag and the risk of collision.*

Mallard

SIZE Body and tail: up to 26 in (65 cm); wingspan: 37 in (95 cm)

RANGE North America, northern Europe, and Asia; introduced in Australia and New Zealand

HABITAT Anywhere near water

FOOD Insects and other small creatures, water plants, seeds, grain

TRACKS AND SIGNS You may see these common ducks feeding tail-up in shallow water. The nest is a shallow dip scraped in the ground and lined with feathers. Duck tracks are smaller than goose and swan tracks but similar in shape. A Mallard track is about 2 in (5 cm) long.

COMMENTS Female Mallards are much plainer than the colorful males, with brownish plumage and some blue feathers on the wings.

Canada Goose

SIZE Body and tail: up to 43 in (110 cm); wingspan: 5½ ft (1.7 m)

RANGE North America; introduced in Europe and New Zealand

HABITAT Tundra, grassland, lakes, meadows, city parks

FOOD Grass, other plants, grain, berries

TRACKS AND SIGNS Look for this large, easily spotted bird on lakes and ponds. It often leaves tracks up to 4 in (10 cm) long on muddy shores. Look for its black head and neck and white cheeks and listen for its honking call. It makes a cup-shaped nest of grass and moss near water and lines it with feathers. Goose tracks show three forward-pointing toes, the webbing between them, and claws. The claw of the smaller backward-pointing toe sometimes shows.

COMMENTS When migrating, these birds fly in V-formation.

Birds of Prey

Most birds of prey, or raptors, are fierce hunters. They range from tiny falcons to huge eagles, but all have excellent eyesight, strong feet with sharp claws, and a hooked beak for tearing prey apart. Owls are raptors, too, but they hunt at night, when other birds of prey are asleep. Birds of prey do not often walk on the ground, so tracks are very rarely seen, but you may find their pellets (*see pages 142–143*) or hear owls hooting in the night.

◄ *Peregrine Falcons, like this one feeding her young, often build their nest high up on cliff faces, out of reach of predators.*

Osprey

SIZE Body and tail: up to 23 in (58 cm); wingspan: 6 ft (1.8 m)
RANGE Almost worldwide
HABITAT Lakes, rivers, coastlines
FOOD Fish, which it snatches from the water with its spiny feet; the spines help the Osprey grip its slippery prey
TRACKS AND SIGNS Look for the Osprey, one of the largest birds of prey in North America, hovering over water looking for fish before plunging feet first to seize its prey. The large nest is made of sticks, usually in a tree or on a rock ledge near water, but sometimes on the ground. Listen for its whistling call. Its tracks are rarely seen as it seldom walks on the ground. Like owls, the Osprey can turn one front toe to face backward.

Peregrine Falcon

SIZE Body and tail: up to 20 in (50 cm); wingspan: 43 in (110 cm)
RANGE Almost worldwide
HABITAT Varied, including mountains and cities
FOOD Mainly birds; also bats, other small mammals
TRACKS AND SIGNS The Peregrine Falcon is sometimes seen in cities now, where it hunts pigeons and other birds. It nests on ledges on cliffs or buildings or it may take over the nest of another large bird. It rarely comes to ground. It has typical four-toed feet, three toes facing forward and one back. All toes are equipped with sharp claws for killing prey.
COMMENTS When making its spectacular dives toward prey, the Peregrine is the fastest animal on the planet, reaching speeds of up to 200 mph (320 km/h).

Barn Owl

SIZE Body and tail: up to 16 in (40 cm); wingspan: 4 ft (1.2 m)
RANGE North and South America, Europe, Africa, Southeast Asia, Australia
HABITAT Open areas including grassland, desert, farmland
FOOD Small mammals such as mice and shrews
TRACKS AND SIGNS You may hear the Barn Owl's screaming or hissing calls. Look for its pellets, too. Owls, like other birds, bring up pellets that contain the fur and bones they cannot digest. Barn Owl pellets are sausage-shaped and gray in color. You may find owl tracks on soft ground. They are up to 3 in (7.5 cm) long and the fourth toe may be turned backward to help it grip prey.
COMMENTS During the day Barn Owls roost in caves, tree hollows, or farm buildings.

Raptor Eggs

The Barn Owl lays 4–7 white eggs, about 1½ in (4 cm) long. The Osprey lays 2–4 eggs about 2¼ in (6 cm) long, which are creamy or pale yellow with brownish speckles. The Peregrine Falcon lays 3 or 4 eggs about 2 in (5 cm) long. They are brown with darker markings.

▼ *This pellet is from a wild Harpy Eagle chick in the Amazon rain forest. It has been pulled apart to reveal that it contains undigested claws and fur from a two-toed sloth.*

Bird Pellets

Bird pellets are easier to identify than their droppings. The pellet's contents are of great interest to the tracker. A bird cannot chew and so just gulps down certain parts of its prey, whether it can digest them or not. The indigestible parts are coughed up once or twice a day in the form of a neat pellet. Pellets are clearly different to mammal scats: they contain easily identifiable things, such as fur, feathers, bone, insect wings, and shells; and they do not smell anything like as bad!

What pellets can tell us

Pellets are valuable clues to bird activity. A pellet on the ground is a sign that a bird is nesting, roosting, or feeding nearby. If you find one, you can examine it to see what it contains and perhaps work out which species produced it. First, note where you found the pellet and sketch or

photograph it. Next, wearing disposable gloves, place the pellet on a surface, such as a plastic tray, and gently pull it apart using tweezers. If it is hard, soak it in water first.

▲ *The pellets of the Rook, a type of crow, contain much plant matter. Look for crow pellets where they forage or near their colonies.*

Which birds produce pellets?

All birds of prey bring up pellets. Owls, particularly, tend to swallow their prey almost whole. Seabirds also tend to swallow indigestible material such as fish bones and shellfish shells. Other pellet producers include storks, herons, kingfishers, crows, and waders. Even songbirds sometimes bring up pellets containing indigestible seeds or pits.

Types of pellet

OWLS Owl pellets are usually gray and, in some owls, are long and sausage-shaped. They may contain fur, feathers, insect bits, such as beetle wing cases, and bones.

OTHER BIRDS OF PREY Pellets of these birds rarely contain bone as they can usually digest the bones of their prey. They also tend to tear their prey into smaller pieces before eating. Their pellets contain fur, feathers, insect parts, beaks, and claws. Sparrowhawk pellets are up to about 1½ in (4 cm) long and contain lots of feathers, while buzzard pellets are generally made up of rodent fur.

CROW FAMILY Crow pellets tend to be egg-shaped and contain lots of plant material and insect parts. There are often stones in crow pellets. Crow pellets are generally about 2 in (4.5 cm) long, while those of Rooks and jackdaws are smaller.

GULLS These may be long or round and contain fish bones, shells, and sometimes plant remains such as fruit pits. Gulls often swallow litter, such as bits of plastic, rubber bands, and string, which turns up in their pellets.

STORKS AND HERONS Storks can digest bone, but their pellets often contain fur, feathers, and insect parts. Heron pellets vary greatly, but are often oval-shaped and may contain fur from prey such as moles and voles.

▶ *This owl pellet contains pieces of bone. Unlike some other birds of prey, owls cannot digest bone.*

Identify the Bird

These pellets come from a range of birds: a buzzard, a heron and a stork, two gulls, a crow and a jackdaw, an owl, and a sparrowhawk. See if you can guess which pellet comes from which bird.

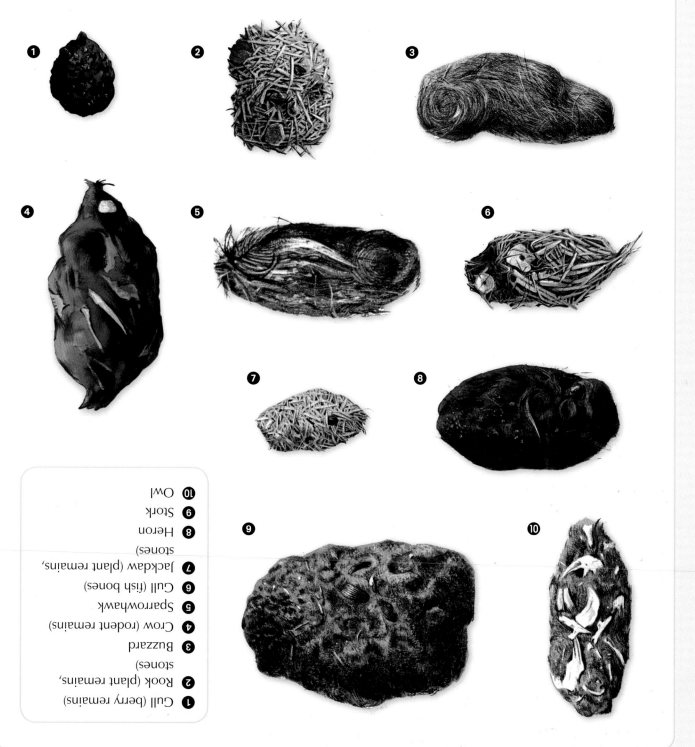

❶ Gull (berry remains)

❷ Rook (plant remains, stones)

❸ Buzzard

❹ Crow (rodent remains)

❺ Sparrowhawk

❻ Gull (fish bones)

❼ Jackdaw (plant remains, stones)

❽ Heron

❾ Stork

❿ Owl

▲ *A Eurasian Oystercatcher has laid its speckled eggs in this simple nest made of twigs on Skomer Island in Wales.*

Waders

Wading birds, such as sandpipers, plovers, and oystercatchers, spend much of their time on coasts or the shores of rivers and lakes, so it is quite common to see their tracks on sand or mud. They usually feed on the ground and have beaks of various lengths and shapes for probing for food to different depths. You may see the holes left by their beaks as they search for small creatures to eat. They are strong fliers, and most are also fast runners.

American Golden Plover

SIZE Body and tail: up to 11 in (28 cm); wingspan: 22 in (57 cm)
RANGE Breeds northern North America; winters South America
HABITAT Tundra, marshes, shorelines, beaches
FOOD Insects, other small creatures, berries, seeds
TRACKS AND SIGNS Look for tracks about 1 in (2.5 cm) long left by plovers as they walk along sandy beaches or muddy shores searching for food. Plovers make a shallow dip on the ground for their nest, lining it with moss and grass.
COMMENTS This bird makes amazing migration journeys of thousands of miles. It breeds during summer in the far north on the tundra, then flies 8,000 miles (12,800 km) south to warmer regions, where it spends the winter months.

Common Redshank

SIZE Body and tail: up to 11 in (28 cm); wingspan: 24 in (62 cm)
RANGE Europe, Asia, Africa
HABITAT Moorland, marshes, estuaries, shores
FOOD Insects, worms, and other small creatures
TRACKS AND SIGNS This is a common bird on shores and in wetland areas, such as marshes and estuaries. Watch for its bright red legs and listen for its very loud, high, whistling call. It nests on the ground in a hollow lined with plants and hidden by tall grasses. Its tracks are about 1¼ in (3 cm) long and sometimes show the back toe.
COMMENTS The Common Redshank feeds with other wading birds and is usually the first to fly off, calling noisily, if disturbed. Its call alerts other birds to possible danger.

Flamingo Feeding Signs

These feeding signs were made in a marsh in the Camargue, France, by the Greater Flamingo. This wader uses filter feeding to obtain its food, treading mud in a circular motion to force small invertebrates out of the mud into the water. It then uses its beak to sieve through the water and scoop up the small creatures. At low tide, these circular imprints remain.

Eurasian Oystercatcher

SIZE Body and tail: up to 18 in (46 cm); wingspan: 32 in (80 cm)

RANGE Europe, Asia, Africa

HABITAT Sea coasts, lakes, rivers, estuaries, beaches, fields

FOOD Mussels, cockles, worms, other small creatures

TRACKS AND SIGNS This oystercatcher species is common and often moves in large flocks, so it should be easy to spot. Like other oystercatchers, this bird has conspicuous black and white plumage and a long red beak. Its nest is a hole in the ground often lined with grass or moss. The tracks are up to 1¾ in (4.5 cm) long.

COMMENTS Oystercatchers use their long beak to prise shellfish such as cockles and mussels off rocks and to open them. Oystercatchers also probe down into mud to catch worms.

Wader Eggs

Plovers usually lay 4 eggs, which are creamy or yellowish in color and marked with brown spots and blotches. They are about 2 in (5 cm) long. The Common Redshank lays 3–5 light brown eggs with darker speckles, which are slightly smaller than plover eggs. Oystercatchers lay 2–4 eggs, usually 3, which are creamy to light brown with darker, brownish-black markings. They are about 2¼ in (5.5 cm) long.

Storks and Herons

Storks are large, long-legged birds with a long neck and broad wings. They do have webbed feet and often feed in water but also search for food on land. They are strong fliers and are easy to spot in the air as they fly with neck and legs stretched out and legs trailing down slightly. Herons, and their relatives egrets and bitterns, are also long-legged birds. They usually find their food by wading in water and grasping prey with their powerful dagger-shaped beaks. Their tracks are large and often seen on shorelines.

▲ *White Storks often build large nests on buildings, including chimneys, church roofs, telegraph poles, and ruins.*

Gray Heron

SIZE Body and tail: up to 36 in (90 cm); wingspan: 6¼ ft (1.9 m)
RANGE Europe, Asia, Africa
HABITAT Very varied but always near water
FOOD Fish is the main food, but it also eats frogs, insects, crabs, and reptiles
TRACKS AND SIGNS Look for this bird at the water's edge at reservoirs, lakes, and rivers. It may also be seen in city parks and yards. Listen for its long, rasping call. Its tracks are about 3 in (7.5 cm) long.
COMMENTS The Gray Heron is very similar to the Great Blue Heron of North America and is the largest heron in Europe.

White Stork

SIZE Body and tail: up to 3½ ft (1.1 m); wingspan: up to 6½ ft (2 m)
RANGE Europe, Asia, Africa
HABITAT Woodland, fields, and near towns and villages
FOOD Very varied, including fish, frogs, insects, lizards, worms, shellfish
TRACKS AND SIGNS This is an unmistakable bird with its large size and red beak and legs. Look for its huge nest, which is made of sticks and built up in a tree or on a building. The White Stork does not make many sounds but does clatter its beak as it changes shifts with its partner at the nest. Its large tracks are 3½ in (8.5 cm) long.
COMMENTS Storks migrate south in winter and may gather in huge flocks.

Great Egret

SIZE Body and tail: up to 3¼ ft
(1 m); wingspan: 4½ ft (1.4 m)
RANGE North and South America,
Europe, Africa, Asia, Australia
HABITAT Marshes, swamps, and other
wetlands; rivers, ponds, lakes
FOOD Very varied, including fish,
shellfish, insects, small mammals, birds
TRACKS AND SIGNS Look for this bird
standing in shallow water with its beak held
ready to snap up prey. Its tracks are about
8 in (20 cm) long and may show claw marks
on the front three toes. The backward-
pointing toe also shows. You may also
hear its deep, croaking call. It makes its nest
in bushes or trees near water.
COMMENTS This is one of the most
widespread of the heron family and can be
seen around most of the world.

◀ SCALE: ⅕ life-size

Stork and Heron Eggs

Herons lay 3–5 eggs, which are a pale blue-green
color and about 2¼ in (6 cm) long. Great Egret
eggs are similar but slightly smaller. The White
Stork lays 3–5 eggs, which are white and up to
2¾ in (7 cm) long.

◀ LIFE-SIZE *footprint of Great Egret*

▲ *A Great Egret laid these three eggs in its large nest
in the Louisiana wetlands.*

Woodpeckers and Nuthatches

Woodpeckers and flickers are well adapted for life in trees. They have strong, sharply clawed feet and a stiff tail that acts as an extra prop to support the bird as it perches. Their tracks are very rarely seen. Woodpeckers feed by hammering into tree trunks with their strong beak to find insects. Nuthatches are another family of tree-living birds. They run up and down tree trunks looking for insects to eat.

▲ *A Great Spotted Woodpecker searches for grubs to eat on a tree trunk.*

Great Spotted Woodpecker

SIZE Body and tail: up to 9 in (23 cm); wingspan: 15 in (39 cm)

RANGE Europe, North Africa, Asia

HABITAT Woodland, parks, backyards

FOOD Beetles and other insects

TRACKS AND SIGNS You are more likely to hear woodpeckers in action than see them. Listen for the fast-paced drumming sound the woodpecker makes when drilling into bark with its beak for insects. Look for holes in tree trunks with beak marks around them. Its tracks are about 2 in (5 cm) long. Woodpeckers also use their beaks to dig nest holes in trees. When looking for a nest, remember that it will appear as a neat hole in soft or decaying wood.

COMMENTS Once the bird has made a feeding hole in a tree or branch, it extends its long tongue inside. The surface of the tongue is sticky, with lots of little barbs, and this makes it easy for the woodpecker to gather mouthfuls of insects.

Northern Flicker

SIZE Body and tail: up to 12 in (30 cm); wingspan: 20 in (50 cm)

RANGE North America, Mexico

HABITAT Woodland, open country, suburban areas

FOOD Ants, other insects, fruit, berries, seeds

TRACKS AND SIGNS This bird spends much of its time on the ground digging for ants and other insects with its strong, sharp beak. It leaves a track similar to the woodpecker's. You may hear it drumming on a tree trunk or a metal roof to mark its territory or attract a mate. Its nest is usually in a tree hole and takes 2 or 3 weeks to dig out. During this time you may find wood chips at the base of the tree.

COMMENTS Like other woodpeckers, the Flicker has a sticky barbed tongue, which helps it gather ants.

Woodpecker and Nuthatch Eggs

The Great Spotted Woodpecker lays 4–7 white eggs, about 1 in (2.5 cm) long. The Northern Flicker lays 6–8 eggs, which are also white and about the same size. Nuthatches lay 5 or 6 white eggs with reddish-brown speckles, just over ½ in (1.5 cm) long. Like those of many hole-nesting birds, the eggs of woodpeckers and nuthatches are white, which helps the parents see them more easily in the dark.

► *Woodpeckers have drilled "wells" into the bark of this willow tree. The birds do this to feed on the tree's sap.*

Red-breasted Nuthatch

SIZE Body and tail: up to 4¼ in (11 cm); wingspan: 8 in (20 cm)

RANGE North America

HABITAT Coniferous forest, mixed woodland, suburban areas

FOOD Insects, spiders, conifer seeds, nuts

TRACKS AND SIGNS This little bird rarely leaves tracks, but if you do find them, they will be about 1½ in (3.5 cm) long. Look for it moving rapidly over tree trunks and branches, searching for insects and seeds. It can even walk down tree trunks headfirst. You may also spot its nest, which is made in a hole in a tree trunk or stump. The hole is smeared with resin from coniferous trees, which may help to keep out predators or competitors.

COMMENTS Nuthatches store excess food in tree holes and on the ground.

Cracking the Nut

Woodpeckers and nuthatches wedge hard food items such as cones, nuts, and fruit stones into cracks or joints in tree bark, logs, and posts. These sites, known as anvils, hold the food firmly while the bird pecks at it. Once the edible part has been eaten, the shell or cone may remain, wedged into the anvil. There may be a pile of debris beneath a frequently used anvil.

▼ *Acorn Woodpeckers drill thousands of holes into a single tree and store acorns in them to eat during winter.*

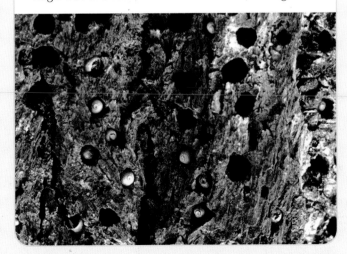

Birds in Your Backyard

Birds are among the easiest of all animals to watch in the wild, and there are ways of attracting them to your own backyard or balcony. Provide the birds with food and water. Perhaps put out some shelters that can be used as nest boxes and roosting sites. And, if you have a yard, keep it as natural as possible. If there are plenty of insects and lots of plant cover, birds are much more likely to visit you. Keep a record of the species you spot and when you saw them, and you might be surprised at the range of different birds that live around you.

Bird feeders

There are all sorts of bird feeders available, including platform-style, freestanding feeders, tube feeders that you can hang in a tree, feeders to hang on a wall, and even some that you can fix to your window with suction cups. Place your feeder carefully, making sure it is easy for you to see from a distance, so you do not frighten the birds away. Check, too, that the feeder is well away from likely predators such as cats. Do not, for example, place a feeder too near a wall or stout branch that a cat could jump from. Make sure feeders are clean and safe for birds. You will find a wide range of types in pet stores.

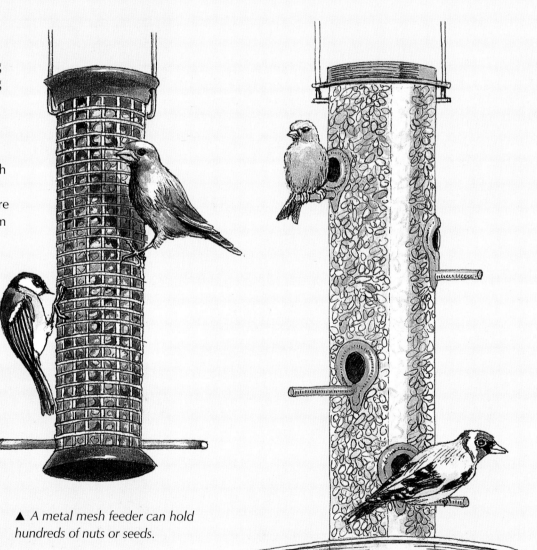

▲ A metal mesh feeder can hold hundreds of nuts or seeds.

▶ Tube feeders allow only birds small enough to enter the holes to reach the seeds inside.

▲ *Weavers, starlings, and doves enjoy a good meal on this bird table near Lake Baringo in Kenya.*

Nesting boxes

Some birds will happily nest in a nesting box if provided. There is a wide range available in different sizes, depending on what kind of birds you are likely to attract in your area. Tits or chickadees, starlings, sparrows, wrens, and even owls will all use nest boxes. Position your nest box very carefully, making sure it is well away from cats and other predators and in a quiet spot where the birds are not likely to be disturbed. Do not put any nesting material in the box—birds prefer to choose their own. But you could leave some material out for them to take, such as pet hair. Clean the box out once a year in the fall when it will be empty.

◀ *Coil feeders are ideal for holding suet balls, which are a good substitute for insects, and for nuts in the shell.*

▶ *Many small birds will nest in a nesting box fastened to a tree well out of the reach of cats.*

Food

You can buy birdseed mixes in pet stores or make your own using sunflower seeds, cracked corn, and white millet. Many birds also enjoy nut mixes, and in winter a fat ball made of suet is a welcome treat. Some birds will also eat scraps such as stale bread, but make sure the bread is not moldy so there is no risk of making the birds ill.

Ground-living Birds

Some birds are so good at running they have given up flying altogether. These flightless birds include some of the biggest of all birds, such as the Ostrich, Emu, rheas, and cassowaries. The birds do have wings, but they are too small to be used for flight. Instead they rely on fast running to escape from danger. Other ground-living birds, such as roadrunners, can fly but prefer to run and spend most of their lives on the ground.

◀ *Emus have large three-toed feet with large claws and run at speeds of up to 30 mph (50 km/h).*

Greater Roadrunner

SIZE Body and tail: up to 21 in (54 cm); wingspan: 19 in (49 cm)
RANGE Southwest U.S.A., Mexico
HABITAT Dry, open country
FOOD Has a very varied diet, including insects, spiders, lizards, snakes, birds and eggs, small mammals, and fruit; it will also eat carrion—animals that are already dead
TRACKS AND SIGNS The Greater Roadrunner and the smaller Lesser Roadrunner of Mexico and Central America are fast runners that can reach speeds of up to 20 mph (32 km/h). Roadrunner tracks are about 3 in (7 cm) long and show four toes, two pointing forward and two backward. The nest is usually made in a thorny bush or cactus. Listen for its cooing call, which gets lower and lower in pitch.
COMMENTS Roadrunners are expert hunters and can kill poisonous creatures such as scorpions and snakes. Sometimes they beat their prey against a rock to kill it.

Emu

SCALE: ¼ life-size ▶

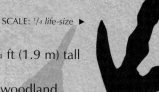

SIZE Body: up to 6¼ ft (1.9 m) tall
RANGE Australia
HABITAT Dry plains, woodland
FOOD Leaves, grass, fruit, insects
TRACKS AND SIGNS The Emu is a fast runner able to speed along at up to 30 mph (50 km/h) on its powerful legs. It may cover up to 10 ft (3 m) in a stride. Look for its nests, which are simply hollows of trampled grass on the ground. Its three-toed tracks are up to 6½ in (17 cm) long.
COMMENTS The Emu is the largest bird in Australia and the second largest in the world—only the Ostrich is bigger.

▶ LIFE-SIZE *Emu track*

Eggs

The female Emu lays a clutch of up to 20 eggs, usually 7–10. These are dark green with a rough pimply surface and measure up to 5½ in (14 cm) in length. Once the eggs are laid, the male takes over and incubates the clutch. Cassowary eggs are lighter green and about the same size. Again, the male incubates the eggs. The Greater Roadrunner lays 2–6 white or cream-colored eggs, which are about 1½ in (4 cm) long.

Southern Cassowary

SIZE Body: up to 6 ft (1.8 m) tall
RANGE Australia and New Guinea
HABITAT Rain forest
FOOD Mainly fruit; also insects, snails, worms
TRACKS AND SIGNS Despite its size, the Southern Cassowary is difficult to spot in dense forest, but you may see signs of trampled vegetation where it has been searching for food to eat. The Southern Cassowary has large feet up to 7 in (18 cm) long. Females generally have larger feet than males. The tracks show three long, forward-pointing toes. The inner toe on each foot has an extra-long claw that measures more than 3 in (8 cm) long.
COMMENTS Never get too close to these large, heavy, powerful birds. They can run at up to 30 mph (50 km/h) and have extremely large, sharp claws on their feet. If threatened, they will leap into the air and kick out with both feet, inflicting serious damage. Cassowaries have been known to kill children and sometimes adults.

Small Songbirds

More than half the world's birds are in the songbird group. Songbirds are also known as perching birds and have feet that are well adapted to their habit of perching on trees and posts. Their feet have four toes, three pointing forward and one backward, and are just the right shape for holding on to slender twigs, reeds, and even wire. The small songbirds are light creatures and leave tracks only on soft surfaces, such as mud or snow.

▲ *A pile of smashed snail shells lying around a hard surface, such as a stone, is a sign of a Song Thrush feeding.*

Common Blackbird

SIZE Body and tail: up to 10 in (25 cm); wingspan: 15 in (38 cm)
RANGE Europe, North Africa, Asia; introduced into Australia and New Zealand
HABITAT Woodland, gardens, parks
FOOD Insects, worms, seeds, berries
TRACKS AND SIGNS Blackbirds are common birds. Look for them after rain, probing the ground for worms or perched on a fence or branch. They usually make their nests in a fork of a tree or shrub or on a ledge or crevice in a wall. The nest is made of plants, grass, and twigs, and is plastered with mud and lined with fine grass. Look for blackbird droppings near food plants. The droppings are often quite liquid and full of fruit seeds. Blackbird tracks are about 2 in (5 cm) long.
COMMENTS Only the male bird is black. The female is dark brown with paler underparts.

European Starling

SIZE Body and tail: up to 9 in (23 cm); wingspan: 16 in (40 cm)
RANGE Europe and Asia, but has been introduced almost worldwide
HABITAT Varied; often farmland, towns, and cities
FOOD Insects, worms and other small creatures, fruit, seeds, and grain
TRACKS AND SIGNS Starlings are common in towns and cities. Look for them perched on buildings or flying in huge flocks in the evening before settling for the night. Their nest is usually made in a hole in a tree or building and is an untidy cup made of stems, leaves, and twigs. The tracks are about 1½ in (4 cm) long.
COMMENTS A little over 100 years ago, about 100 European starlings were released in New York City. About 200 million starlings now live in North America, and they are all descended from this original population.

◀ *This nest, a deep cup of interwoven twigs, belongs to a Red-winged Blackbird, a very common bird in North America. It builds its nest either in a shrub or attached to sturdy stems, often above water.*

American Robin

SIZE Body and tail: up to 11 in (28 cm); wingspan: 16 in (40 cm)

RANGE North America, Mexico

HABITAT Forest, woodland, parks, gardens; often seen in towns and suburban areas

FOOD Worms and other small creatures, as well as fruit

TRACKS AND SIGNS You will often see this bird scurrying around searching for earthworms and then pulling them up out of the ground with a sharp tug. The nest is usually in a tree and made of grass, twigs, and mud. The robin's tracks are about 1½ in (4 cm) long. Listen for this bird's musical, whistling call and also a sharp "chup chup" sound.

COMMENTS This is a very common yard bird that is happy to live near humans. The male's bright red breast makes him easy to spot. The female's plumage is duller and paler.

Songbird Eggs

The Blackbird usually lays about 4–5 eggs, which are about 1¼ in (3 cm) long and colored light blue with mottled, sometimes reddish-brown markings. European Starlings usually lay 5–7 eggs, which are blue or greenish-white and are just over 1 in (2.5 cm) long. The American Robin lays 2–5 light blue eggs, which are also just over 1 in (2.5 cm) long.

Seabirds

Seabirds are some of the most powerful fliers of all birds, and many travel long distances over the ocean as they search for food. Some spend nearly all their time in the air, only coming to land to mate, lay eggs, and rear their young. Seabirds are very good swimmers, and some can also dive. Their feathers form a dense, waterproof cover to protect them from cold and wet. You can see and hear squawking gulls in cities and built-up areas where they scavenge for food. Look for seabird tracks on sandy beaches and muddy shores.

▲ Like many seabirds, these Peruvian Boobies nest on cliffs, where their white droppings are highly visible.

Herring Gull

SIZE Body and tail: up to 26 in (66 cm); wingspan: 4½ ft (1.4 m)
RANGE North America, Europe, northern Asia
HABITAT Coasts, estuaries, mudflats, also urban areas
FOOD Fish, shellfish, insects, birds, eggs; also takes food from garbage cans and dumps
TRACKS AND SIGNS You will see these large birds in any coastal areas, including cities, and hear their loud, chuckling calls. Very bold, they will scavenge around picnic sites, restaurants, and cafés. Do not get too close as they have big, sharp beaks. The nest is a simple scrape on the ground or a cliff ledge. The tracks are around 2 in (5 cm) long. Gull pellets (see pages 142–143) are a common sign.
COMMENTS Young Herring Gulls are dark brown. They do not have adult plumage until they are three years old.

Brown Pelican

SIZE Body and tail: up to 4½ ft (1.3 m); wingspan 6½ ft (2 m)
RANGE U.S.A., Caribbean, South America
HABITAT Coasts and estuaries
FOOD Fish and other sea creatures
TRACKS AND SIGNS This pelican is easy to identify. It is the only pelican with brown feathers and the only one that dives from the air into the water to catch its food. Look for its spectacular plunges with wings held back and neck curved into an S-shape. It nests in colonies. The nest is made of sticks and built in low trees or on the ground. Its track is about 6 in (15 cm) long and shows four clawed toes.
COMMENTS If you see a Brown Pelican standing still, it might be incubating its eggs. Brown Pelicans do not sit on their eggs to keep them warm, like most birds do. Instead, they warm them using their webbed feet.

Great Cormorant

SIZE Body and tail: up to 35 in (90 cm); wingspan 5¼ ft (1.6 m)

RANGE Eastern North America, Europe, Africa, Asia, Australia

HABITAT Coasts, marshes, lakes

FOOD Fish

TRACKS AND SIGNS You may spot these birds bobbing on the water then diving in search of prey. Look for them perched on rocks with wings spread out to dry after hunting. Cormorants nest in huge groups called colonies. Patches of bare ground under trees may be a sign of nesting cormorants—large amounts of their liquid droppings kill off plant life. Their four-toed tracks show claws and are up to 5 in (12.5 cm) long.

COMMENTS Cormorants are expert underwater hunters that dive from the surface and swim at high speed to catch their prey.

Seabird Eggs

The Herring Gull lays 1–3 pale olive green or brownish eggs with dark brown speckles. The eggs are about 2¾ in (7 cm) long. Cormorant eggs are pale bluish-green with a rough, chalky white covering. The Great Cormorant usually lays 3–5 eggs, which are 2½ in (6.5 cm) long. The Brown Pelican lays a clutch of about 3 large white eggs, 3 in (7.5 cm) long.

◄ *A Herring Gull watches over its clutch of three eggs. Gulls make simple nests like this on the ground, on cliffs, and on buildings.*

Birds' Nests

Birds make nests to keep their eggs and young warm and safe, not for sleeping in. Most birds sleep in trees, tree holes, or on ledges—in fact, anywhere they can get some shelter and protection—and build nests only in the breeding season. Often, both partners build the nest together, or one builds while the other brings material to use. But with some birds, including thrushes, the female builds the nest alone. Nests can be easier to spot in winter, when many trees are bare of leaves. Look again in spring when the occupants may return.

Types of Nest

The simplest nests are just scrapes in the ground or on a cliff ledge, sometimes lined with feathers or twigs. Many seabirds make scrape nests like these, as do many ducks. Other birds build platforms of twigs and plants, sometimes on water or among reeds. Trees are very popular nest sites with a wide variety of birds. Nests made in trees include ball-shaped and cup-shaped nests and carefully woven pouch nests, such as those of penduline tits. Swifts and martins use mud and saliva to bind nest material together and make small, cuplike structures on cliffs or cave walls. Other birds nest in holes: for example, kingfishers dig a nest tunnel in a riverbank and woodpeckers excavate a hole in a tree.

▶ *A Northern Flicker looks out from the hole it has dug out for its nest in a tree trunk.*

◀ *Song Thrushes lay their eggs in cup-shaped nests made of twigs, grass, and moss and thickly lined with mud and dung.*

Nest watch

It's fun to look for birds' nests, but you should never disturb any you find or the parents may desert the nest and their eggs or young. Do not touch the nest, just keep an eye on it from a safe distance. You may see the parents coming and going, perhaps the male bringing food for the female while she keeps the eggs warm, or, later, both parents working hard to keep their young well fed. If you can, keep a journal of what you see and take pictures from a distance. Check the same site the following spring to see if your birds have returned.

Identifying nests

EAGLES Eagles make some of the largest of all birds' nests. They are built on rock ledges or in trees and are made of branches and twigs.

COOT A coot makes a platform nest of leaves and stems among reeds in or by shallow water.

KINGFISHER A kingfisher digs a tunnel in the riverbank with a nest chamber at the end.

CHAFFINCH The Chaffinch makes a cup of moss, grass, roots, and feathers held together with spider web silk.

KITTIWAKE A kittiwake is a kind of gull. It generally nests on cliff ledges, where it is very difficult for predators to reach its eggs or young. The nest is usually made of grass, mud, and seaweed.

STORK Storks nest on trees or buildings, making a large nest of sticks, branches, and other plant matter. The nest may be used year after year.

RED-NECKED GREBE The Red-necked Grebe makes its nest in lakes or slow-moving rivers. The nest is made of plant material and either floats on the water surface or is anchored to aquatic plants.

WOODPECKER A woodpecker uses its strong beak to make a hole in a tree for its nest.

MARTIN Some species of martin nest on walls or ceiling alcoves of buildings, especially outside beneath the roof eaves, using their saliva to glue the nest to the surface.

◄ *From top to bottom: a Bald Eagle's tree nest; Black-legged Kittiwakes on a cliff nest; a Red-necked Grebe's river nest.*

Insects and Other Invertebrates

Insects and other invertebrates do not have backbones like birds and mammals do. Instead, many have a hard shell or a tough outer covering to protect the soft parts of their body. Invertebrates make up more than 95 percent of all known animal species. Only a few invertebrates leave footprints but there are plenty of other signs to discover. Look for the slime trails left by slugs and snails and for the silken webs made by spiders. Search the beach for shells of creatures such as crabs, clams, and mussels. You might spot wasps' and ants' nests in woodland, the skins of molting dragonfly nymphs left near ponds, or leaves chewed by caterpillars.

◀ *This Canopy Jumping Spider is about the size of your thumbnail. Its eight eyes give it excellent vision. When it hunts, it stalks its prey before leaping up to 50 times the length of its own body to sink its fangs into its victim.*

Crustaceans and Worms

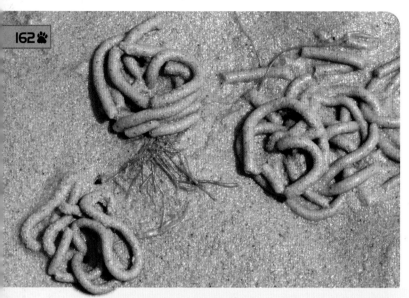

The crustacean group includes a wide variety of sea creatures, such as barnacles, crabs, lobsters, and shrimp, as well as land dwellers such as the woodlouse. Most have a tough outer skeleton to protect the soft body inside and several pairs of legs. Worms belong to a separate group. There are lots of kinds of worm in the sea, and the earthworm lives in woods and gardens all over the world.

◀ *These worm casts left on a beach at low tide were formed by sand that has passed through the worms' bodies.*

Edible Crab

SIZE Body: up to 11 in (28 cm) wide
RANGE North Atlantic coasts
HABITAT Lower shore and around rocks and rock pools
FOOD Other smaller crustaceans and mollusks as well as bits of fish left by other animals
TRACKS AND SIGNS Look for tracks left by the sideways movement of the crab on its four pairs of walking legs. Crabs molt their shells and grow new ones as they get bigger, so you will often see old shells the crab has outgrown on the shoreline.
COMMENTS Crabs use their first pair of legs for feeding, not walking. These legs are tipped with powerful pincers for breaking open the shells of prey such as mollusks.

Acorn Barnacle

SIZE Body: up to $^5/_8$ in (1.5 cm) across
RANGE North Atlantic coasts
HABITAT Rocks and other hard surfaces on the shore
FOOD Microscopic plants (plankton) that the barnacle filters from the water
SIGNS Barnacles are common on the seashore in areas that are covered at high tide. Look on rocks, piers, and breakwaters, and you will see large groups of barnacles. They even take up residence on other shellfish such as mussels.
COMMENTS Barnacles feed when covered by water. A "trap door" in the top of the shell opens, and the barnacle extends its feathery limbs to gather plankton from the water. When the tide is out, the barnacle stays firmly closed.

Hermit Crab

If you spot what seems to be a snail or periwinkle moving surprising quickly across a beach or rock pool, you may have found a hermit crab. The hermit crab does not have a hard shell to protect its soft body, so it takes the discarded shell of another creature, such as a snail. The crab lives inside the shell and reaches out with its sharp pincers to grab food. Sea anemones often live on a hermit crab's shell, feeding on the crab's leftovers and scaring off predators.

▶ *This hermit crab has found an empty shell to protect it from predators.*

Woodlouse

SIZE Body: up to 3/8 in (1 cm) long
RANGE Worldwide
HABITAT Damp dark places, such as under stones and crevices in walls
FOOD Rotting plants and fungi
SIGNS Lift up a plant pot or stone in any backyard or park, or a rotting branch in a wood, and you will probably see woodlice scurrying around.
COMMENTS A woodlouse has seven pairs of legs. As it grows, it has to shed the skeleton or shell on the outside of its body and grow a new one. It sheds its shell in two parts—first the back half, then the front.

Earthworm

SIZE Body: up to 12 in (30 cm) long, although there are also much larger giant earthworms in Africa and Australia
RANGE Worldwide
HABITAT Surface layers of soil in fields, woods, and yards
FOOD Dead leaves and other plant materials, as well as soil
SIGNS Look for worms after heavy rain, when they may crawl to the soil surface. Keep an eye out, too, for worm "casts" on the ground. These are little worm-shaped piles of soil and plant material that have passed through the worm's body and been excreted. The worm's activity is good for soil, breaking the soil up and helping to get air and water into it. You may also see the earthworm's tracks, like a line in the soil.
COMMENTS Many birds love to eat worms and are good at finding them. Watch a blackbird on a field or in your yard. It will walk over the grass then suddenly plunge its beak into the earth and pull up a worm.

▲ *At low tide, look for tide pools like this one, filled with sea creatures such as mussels, barnacles, and starfish.*

Mollusks

Slugs and snails are some of the most familiar land-living mollusks, but the greatest range is found in the sea and on seashores. These include creatures such as mussels, limpets, periwinkles, and clams. In most mollusks the body is divided into three parts—the head, which contains the mouth and sense organs, the body, and the foot, a fleshy part of the body on which the animal moves along. Most, but not all, mollusks have a tough shell that protects the soft body. Look for mollusk shells washed up on the seashore.

Common Mussel

SIZE Body: up to 4 in (10 cm) long
RANGE Cool coastal waters worldwide
HABITAT Rocks and other surfaces
FOOD Tiny plants and animals (plankton) filtered from the water
SIGNS Look for clumps of mussels on rocks and in rock pools. You will also find broken and empty shells among seaweed and other debris on the seashore.
COMMENTS Look carefully and you will see the strong threads that attach the mussel to its rocky home. These threads are made inside the mussel's body.

Scallop

SIZE Body: up to 4 in (10 cm) long
RANGE Atlantic and Pacific oceans
HABITAT Sandy and gravel-bottomed coastal waters down to about 1,000 ft (300 m) deep
FOOD Tiny plants and animals (plankton) filtered from the water
SIGNS Look for the almost circular shells washed up on seashores.
COMMENTS A scallop swims by clapping its shells together, forcing out jets of water that push it forward.

▶ *Apple snails live in water and use gills to breathe. They also have lungs for breathing in air when they come on to land to lay eggs on plant stems and when food is scarce in the water.*

Slugs

Slugs are mollusks like snails, but they do not have external shells. Like snails, slugs make slimy mucus in their body, which helps them glide over the ground. Look for the slug's glistening silvery trails. Slugs eat large amounts of leaves and other plant material and some species can be a nuisance to gardeners.

Razor Clam

SIZE Body: up to 10 in (25 cm) long
RANGE Atlantic and Pacific coasts
HABITAT Sandy-bottomed shallow water
FOOD Tiny plants and animals (plankton), which the clam filters from the water
SIGNS Razor clams live in burrows on sandy shores below the low-tide line. Look for the holes in the sand that may be a sign of a razor clam's burrow. Some razor clam burrows are just little dips in the sand, but others have raised sides. If you dig very quickly, you might uncover a clam, but clams can dig quickly too. They sometimes squirt water or sand out of the hole, so watch out!
COMMENTS This clam's long, razor-shaped shell is often washed up on seashores.

Garden Snail

SIZE Body: up to 3½ in (9 cm) long
RANGE Europe (similar species in North America and elsewhere)
HABITAT Farmland, fields, gardens—anywhere with plant life
FOOD Leaves and fruit, but will also eat dead insects and other small creatures
TRACKS AND SIGNS Look for the snail's slimy trail. It produces mucus in its body to help it move along the ground more easily and protect itself against rough surfaces. The evening and after rain are good times to look for signs of snail activity.
COMMENTS Most snails spend the day inside their shell and come out at night to find food. Lots of birds like to eat snails, and you often find empty shells.

Spiders and Scorpions

Spiders and scorpions are not insects. They belong to a separate group of invertebrate animals called arachnids. Most arachnids have four pairs of legs and do not have wings or antennae. All spiders can make silk using special glands at the end of the body, although not all make webs. Scorpions have a sting at the end of the body, which they use to kill prey and defend themselves from enemies.

▲ *Nursery web spiders place their newly hatched babies in a web hanging from a plant. Look for nursery webs in your yard.*

Scorpion

SIZE Body: up to 7 in (18 cm) long; most species are about 2–5 in (5–10 cm)
RANGE Worldwide, usually in warmer areas
HABITAT Very varied, including desert, grassland, woodland, rain forest
FOOD Insects, but the largest scorpions may also prey on lizards, snakes, and small mammals such as mice
TRACKS AND SIGNS Scorpions are usually active at night and spend the day in dark, hidden places, such as under logs, rocks, and other objects, in crevices in buildings, even inside shoes! Never get too near these creatures as some have a deadly sting. You may occasionally see scorpion tracks in sand, sometimes with drag marks of the tail between the tiny footprints.
COMMENTS Female scorpions carry their young, miniature versions of the adults, on their backs until they are big enough to survive by themselves.

Apart from their size, scorpion tracks are quite similar from species to species. ▼

Crab Spider

SIZE Body: up to 3/8 in (1 cm) long
RANGE Worldwide, there are several thousand species
HABITAT Very varied: fields, yards, woodland
FOOD Insects
SIGNS These spiders do not spin webs but lie in wait for their prey. Some sit on flowers, waiting for flower-feeding insects to approach. Look carefully and you may see a brightly colored spider that almost exactly matches the petals it is sitting on.
COMMENTS Not all crab spiders are colorful. Some hunt their prey on the ground and are dull brown or black so they can hide in soil and dead leaves.

European Garden Spider

SIZE Body: up to ¾ in (2 cm) long
RANGE Europe and North America, but there are very similar species worldwide
HABITAT Yards, parks
FOOD Flies and other insects
SIGNS These spiders build webs between plants and attached to buildings and other backyard structures. You may see clusters of eggs attached to a leaf or twig beside the web.
COMMENTS Once the spider has caught its prey, it wraps it in threads of silk so it cannot escape.

Trapdoor Spider

SIZE Body: up to 2 in (5 cm) long
RANGE Southern U.S.A., South America, southern Europe, South Africa, Asia, Australia
HABITAT On the ground in burrows made on sloping banks, grassy meadows, woodland
FOOD Insects
SIGNS Trapdoor spiders live in a burrow they dig in the soil. The entrance to the burrow is made of soil and silk and hinged with silk so it opens easily. The entrances are very well camouflaged, but if you suspect these spiders are around, you may be able to find a trapdoor entrance on the ground. The trapdoor is usually round or D-shaped.
COMMENTS The spider waits inside its burrow. It senses the movements of insects on the ground above, pops out of its door, and pulls the prey into its burrow.

Baby Spiders

▼ *This nursery web spider is carrying her egg sac, a casing she makes out of silk to protect her eggs.*

Most spiders produce large numbers of young. In summer you may spot clumps of baby spiders huddled together in a bush or against a wall. Eventually they need to split up in order to find enough food, and they do this by means of a process called ballooning. The spider stands with the tip of its body pointing upward and spins a thread of silk. This catches the breeze and the spider is carried away as though on a parachute. Look for these tiny spiders' silken threads, which land on plants.

Spiders' Webs

Spiders are among the few creatures that build traps to catch their prey, and spiders' webs are among the most obvious of all invertebrate animal signs. All spiders produce silk, but they use their silk to catch prey in many different ways, not just by making webs. Ogre-faced spiders make a small, strong net of silk that they hold between their front legs. If prey comes near, the spider quickly holds up the net so the prey flies into it. Spitting spiders catch their victims by spitting out a sticky substance from glands near their mouth. This falls over the prey and pins it down.

Making an Orb Web

The webs most often seen in our houses and yards are made by orb weavers. There are many species of these spiders living all over the world. Spiders can make two types of silk. One type hardens into a tough, non-sticky thread and is used for the outer parts of the web. The other is sticky and is used for the center.

1

2 It then adds spokes and spins a widely spaced, non-sticky spiral. This spiral keeps the spokes separated so the spider can add the final part of the web.

Sticky spiral (red) to trap prey

1 An orb-weaving spider starts by making a framework of non-sticky silk threads, attaching them to plants or other supports with the help of the breeze. It then crawls along them, spinning more silk to add strength.

3 The spider then spins the sticky central spiral that will trap prey, removing the non-sticky spiral as it goes. It leaves non-sticky spokes in place so that it can walk along them without becoming stuck. It waits nearby for prey to fly into its web.

3

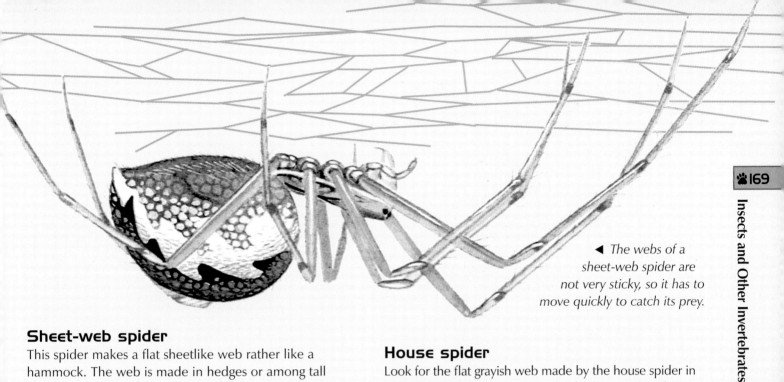

◄ *The webs of a sheet-web spider are not very sticky, so it has to move quickly to catch its prey.*

Sheet-web spider

This spider makes a flat sheetlike web rather like a hammock. The web is made in hedges or among tall grass and may measure as much as 12 in (30 cm) across. Silken threads above the web hold it in place, and if a prey hits one of these threads, it tumbles down onto the web. The spider, which waits below, then grabs the prey and quickly ties it up with more silk. Sheet webs are very easy to spot, particularly when they are sparkling with dew on summer mornings.

Water Spider

The Water or Diving Bell Spider makes a special underwater home that works like a diving bell, allowing the spider to breathe air. It is the only spider that spends its whole life in water. The spider starts by spinning a bell-shaped shelter of silk, which is attached to water plants. It then supplies this with bubbles of air collected at the water's surface.

When the bell is complete, the spider sits inside waiting for prey to come near. It pounces on its prey and brings it into the bell to eat. You may be able to spot these spiders and their homes near water plants in shallow ponds.

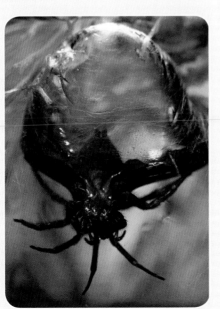

▶ *A Water Spider emerges from its underwater air bell.*

House spider

Look for the flat grayish web made by the house spider in little-disturbed corners of garages, sheds, or attics. The spider waits below its web for prey to become tangled up in the sticky strands.

▲ *A Black-and-yellow Garden Spider eats the prey caught in its web. It is also called the Writer Spider, because the thick strands in the center of its web reminded people of writing.*

Butterflies and Moths

Butterflies and moths live wherever plants grow, and there are thousands of different species. All have two pairs of wings covered in tiny scales, which are sometimes brightly colored. Most have a tubelike mouth for sucking up liquid food such as nectar. A young butterfly or moth is called a caterpillar. A caterpillar spends most of its time feeding on plants and grows very fast.

▲ Moth cocoons are often attached to trees but may be well camouflaged and tricky to spot. This cocoon belongs to the Cecropia Moth, the largest moth in North America.

Small Cabbage White

SIZE Wingspan: up to 2 in (5 cm)
RANGE Europe, North Africa, Asia; introduced into North America and Australia
HABITAT Fields and yards
FOOD Adults feed on plant nectar; caterpillars eat cabbage and cauliflower leaves and garden plants such as nasturtiums
SIGNS Look for the green caterpillars on food plants and for the pupae, which may be green or brown.
COMMENTS Males of this species of cabbage white have one small dark spot on each front wing. Females have two.

Monarch Butterfly

SIZE Wingspan: up to 4 in (10 cm)
RANGE North America
HABITAT Fields and roadsides where milkweed plant grows
FOOD Caterpillars eat milkweed leaves and buds
SIGNS Wherever you see milkweed plants, look for Monarch Butterflies and their caterpillars and eggs. The eggs are laid on the underside of leaves, and the caterpillars are ringed with black, yellow, and white stripes. You may also see their green pupae hanging from leaves.
COMMENTS Every fall millions of Monarch Butterflies make an amazing migration south, traveling as far as 2,000 miles (3,000 km) to Mexico. The following spring they make their way north, laying their eggs as they go.

Oleander Sphinx Moth

SIZE Wingspan: up to 4¾ in (12 cm)

RANGE Europe, Africa, southern Asia

HABITAT Backyards, parks, woodland

FOOD Caterpillars feed on oleander and periwinkle leaves

SIGNS Look for the large caterpillar, which can be up to 6 in (15 cm) long and is green with blue eyespots on the third segment. The pupa is brown and usually found on the ground.

COMMENTS The caterpillar's eyespots can trick an enemy into thinking the caterpillar is bigger than it really is.

▲ Caterpillars eat a lot and leave droppings on or beneath the plants they eat. The dark pellets left by this Death's Head Hawkmoth caterpillar are similar to those of many species.

Egg to Adult

Butterflies and moths usually lay their eggs on plants. The eggs hatch into young called caterpillars, which start munching on plants as soon as they hatch. The caterpillar grows fast and sheds its skin several times as it gets bigger. When the caterpillar is fully grown, it stops feeding and moving, attaches itself to vegetation (or sometimes buries itself), and becomes a pupa, forming a hard protective coating around itself. Many moths also spin a silk casing called a cocoon around the pupa. Inside, it makes its magical transformation from a wingless larva to a winged adult.

▶ A Monarch Butterfly emerges fully formed from its pupal casing.

Termites and Ants

Ants live in huge groups of thousands of individuals, called colonies. Most colonies make a nest of interconnecting tunnels in rotting wood or under the ground. Each colony includes at least one queen ant, and she lays all of the eggs. The workers do all the work of the colony, gathering food and looking after eggs and young. Termites are not related to ants, although their habits are similar. They build large nests with special chambers for eggs and young and for food storage.

▲ A group of leafcutter ants struggles back to their nest, carrying pieces of leaf much larger than themselves.

Leafcutter Ant

SIZE Body: workers are up to ½ in (1.2 cm) long, but the queen may be 1 in (2.5 cm) long
RANGE Central and South America
HABITAT Rain forest, woodland
FOOD Fungus that the ants grow on their compost heaps
SIGNS Leafutter ants cut pieces of leaves and carry them back to their nest, where they use them to feed the fungus they grow. Look for ants carrying large pieces of leaf and for leaves with sections cut out of them. You may also see piles of earth near the entrance to the ants' nest.
COMMENTS A leafcutter ant can carry a piece of leaf weighing 10 times its own weight.

Carpenter Ant

SIZE Body: workers are up to ½ in (1.2 cm) long, but the queen may be 1 in (2.5 cm) long
RANGE Worldwide (there are many different species)
HABITAT Forest, woodland, houses; they make their nests in wood
FOOD Insects; also feed on meat and sweet things inside houses, such as honey, sugar, and jam. They do not eat wood.
SIGNS Carpenter ants tunnel in wood to make nests. Signs of their presence include little piles of shredded wood that they have dug out to make tunnels and nest chambers. Listen, too, for rustling sounds coming from inside areas such as baseboards.
COMMENTS These ants can do a great deal of damage to wood in buildings.

Termite

SIZE Body: most are under 1 in (2.5 cm) long; queens can be 5 in (12.5 cm) or more in length

RANGE Worldwide in warm and tropical areas

HABITAT Varied, including grassland, woodland, rain forest

FOOD Wood is the main food of many termites, but some species eat grass and other plants

SIGNS Termites build large nests, some underground, some like huge towers above the surface. They also make big round nests in trees. Look for the covered runways they make on the tree trunk and across branches leading to the nest. These are made of earth and saliva. If part of the runway is damaged, the termites quickly repair it.

COMMENTS Some termites feed on fungus that they grow in special "fungus gardens" inside the nest.

▲ Some termites make nests like this one high up in a tree, out of reach of many predators.

Ant Families

No ant lives alone. They all live in colonies—huge groups of thousands of insects. The colony is headed by the queen, who is much larger than all the rest and lays the eggs for the colony. There is more than one queen in some colonies. The rest of the females are workers, and they build the nest, gather food, and care for the young. Once a year the ant colony produces winged males and females, which fly out from the nest and mate. After mating, the males die and the mated females lose their wings and set up colonies.

▶ These examples of different "castes," or ranks, of wood ant are typical of many ant species. In some types of ants there are different sizes of worker and also soldier ants, which are specialist fighters with extra large head and jaws.

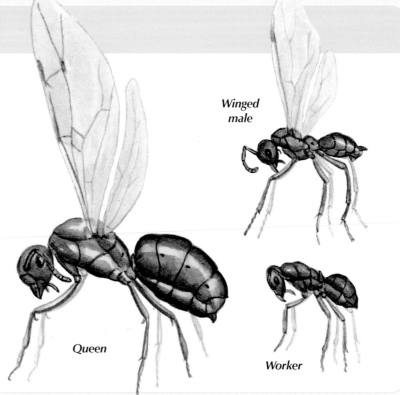

Winged male

Queen

Worker

Wasps and Bees

There are thousands of different kinds of bees and wasps, and you can see them all over the world. They vary greatly in appearance, but they all have two pairs of wings, and most have a long body with a definite "waist." Some, such as leafcutter bees and mud dauber wasps, live alone and make their own nests for their young. Others, such as honeybees and common wasps, live in huge groups called colonies and build elaborate nests.

◄ *Paper wasps chew wood fibers to make a gray or brown papery material, which they use to build their nests.*

Leafcutter Bee

SIZE Body: up to ¾ in (2 cm) long
RANGE Worldwide (there are many different kinds)
HABITAT Yards, fields, orchards, woods
FOOD Flower nectar
SIGNS This type of bee cuts pieces from leaves and uses them to line the cells in its nest. Stores of nectar and pollen are put into the cells, and an egg is laid in each one. Look for leaves with neat circles cut out of them, then watch for the leafcutter bee in action.
COMMENTS Although this bee does damage leaves, it also pollinates plants as it flies from one to another feeding on nectar.

Gall Wasp

SIZE Body: up to ½ in (1.2 cm) long
RANGE Worldwide
HABITAT Forests, woods, parks, yards
Many gall wasps live in and around oak trees
FOOD The adult wasp feeds on plant nectar; its young (larvae) eat the galls (see below)
SIGNS These wasps lay their eggs on the leaves, buds, and twigs of a tree, and a round swelling, called a gall, forms around each egg. When the young wasp (larva) hatches, it feeds on the inside of the gall. Look for these galls, which you will often see on the underside of oak leaves.
COMMENTS Galls can be up to 2 in (5 cm) across, but most are much smaller. Some gall wasps lay their eggs on rose plants.

Gall

Honeybee

SIZE Body: up to ½ in (1.2 cm) long. Queen is larger at about ¾ in (2 cm)

RANGE Now worldwide

HABITAT Fields, yards, parks, open woodland; nests in hollow trees and in hives provided by beekeepers

FOOD Adults feed on flower nectar; larvae (young bees) eat honey and royal jelly, a very nutritious substance made by worker bees

SIGNS Watch for honeybees flying from flower to flower to collect nectar. If you look carefully—without getting too close—you will see the yellow pollen grains on the bee's legs.

COMMENTS There are three types of honeybee. The ones you see busily gathering nectar and pollen are worker bees, which are all female. Back at the hive are the queen, who is the head of the colony and lays the eggs, and some male drones, who mate with the queen.

Common Wasp

SIZE Body: up to ¾ in (2 cm) long

RANGE North America, Europe, North Africa, Asia; introduced in Australia and New Zealand

HABITAT Very varied, including yards, meadows, woodland

FOOD Adults feed mainly on nectar and fruit, as well as some carrion—dead animals; they catch insects to feed to their young

SIGNS Look for wasps around fruit trees, on flowers, and buzzing around your picnic. Watch to see where they fly, and you may spot their nest. But do not go too close or you may get stung.

COMMENTS Common Wasps, like many other types of wasp, build their nest from a papery material made from chewed wood mixed with saliva. The nest is made in a hole in the ground or sometimes in a shed, attic, or under the eaves of a roof.

Inside the Hive

A honeybee nest, or hive, contains a number of long wax structures made up of six-sided cells. These structures are called combs and may be inside a tree hole or an artificial hive. The cells contain eggs or larvae (young bees) or food stores of honey or pollen. Queen bees are raised in special long cells, which hang from the lower edge of combs. When a bee gets back from a food-gathering trip, other bees gather round to collect the stores and pack them into cells.

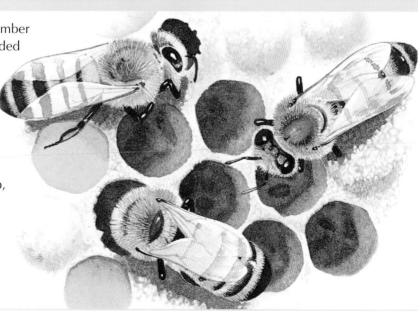

▶ *Honeybees build six-sided cells like these, where they store food and keep their eggs.*

Insect Builders

Insects, such as ants, bees, wasps, and termites, make some of the most amazing of all animal nests. They build structures to shelter colonies that sometimes contain thousands of individuals and provide a safe place to rear young. And the little ant lion is one of the very few insects that builds a trap to catch its prey.

Inside a Termite Nest

Some termites build mounds that tower 25 ft (7.6 m) above the ground. But the living areas are all below ground. There are chambers for the young termites (larvae), a special cell for the queen termite, and food storage areas. This type of termite also grows special fungus, which the insects eat and feed to their young, and these "fungus gardens" are also below ground. Tunnels lead from the nest to the surface. Above the nest, the huge tower acts like a kind of air-conditioning system. Chimneys in the tower maintain an even temperature within the nest.

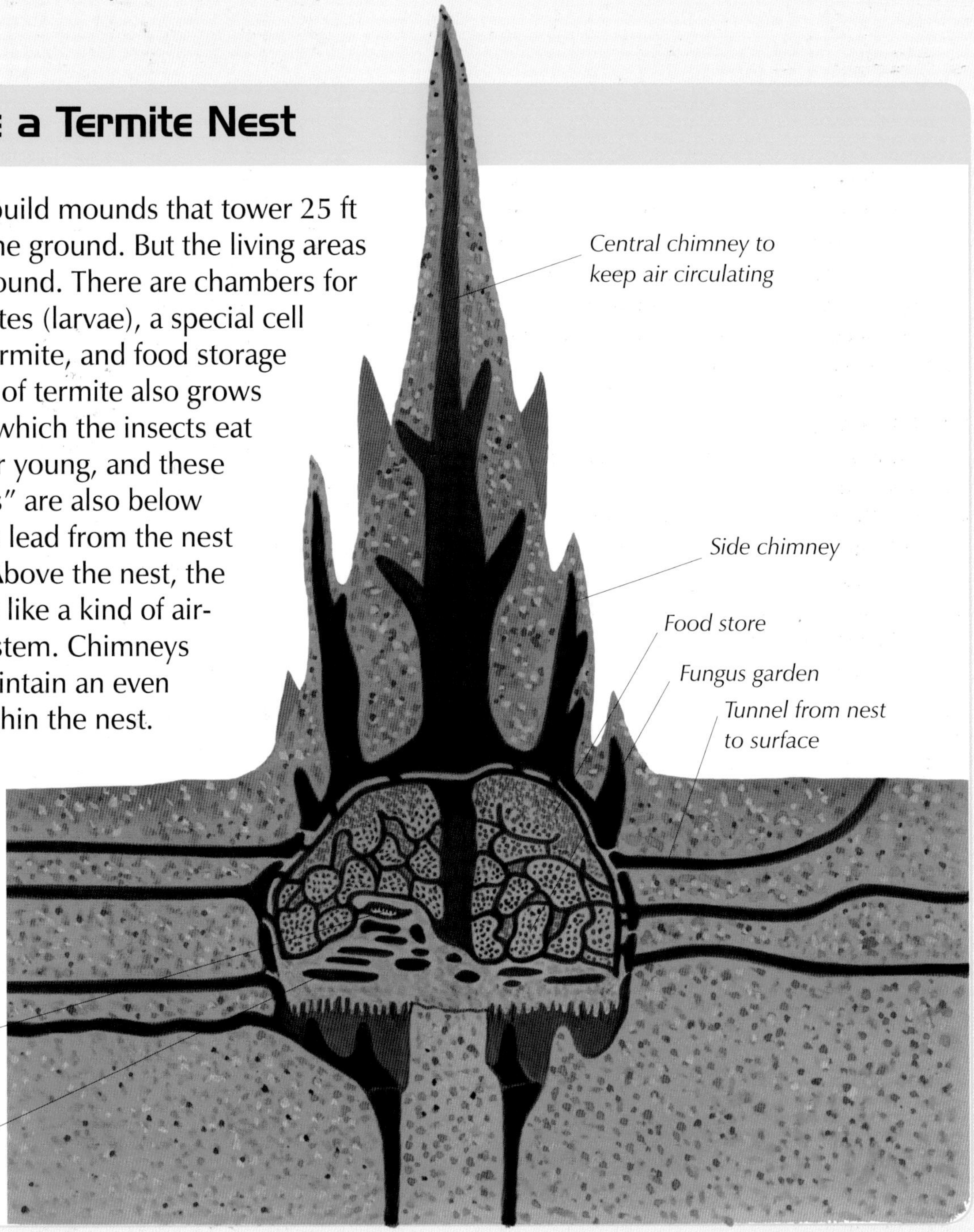

Central chimney to keep air circulating

Side chimney

Food store

Fungus garden

Tunnel from nest to surface

▶ The huge tower on a termite mound keeps the living quarters below well ventilated.

Cell for queen termite

Chamber for larvae (young termites)

Ants' nest

One of the easiest insect nests is to find is the moundlike home of the red wood ant. It is several feet high and is often made in a woodland around a tree stump, which helps to support it. Inside is a network of passages and chambers for eggs and larvae, which usually extends underground as well as into the mound itself. Twigs, grass, and pine needles cover the mound, and you may notice trails of ants coming and going from the nest.

Potter wasp

Potter wasps, or mud daubers, live alone, not in large colonies. The female builds a pot-shaped nest of mud and water on the ground or on a wall or branch. Inside there may be a number of cells. She places an egg in each cell and adds food such as caterpillars or other larvae, which she has stung and paralyzed. The chamber is then sealed. When the wasp larva hatches, it eats the food left for it, then breaks out of the chamber.

▲ *A female potter wasp makes her mud nest in the Arabian Desert.*

◀ *Wood ants have made this large nest out of pine needles.*

The ant lion's trap

The ant lion is not an ant at all, but a relative of lacewings and alderflies. The adult looks rather like a dragonfly, but the larva is wingless, with large, spiny jaws. The larva digs a pit in sandy soil to catch prey, waiting in a tiny hole at the bottom for passing insects to enter the pit. Once on the pit's slopes, the prey slips and slides downward. When it reaches the bottom, the ant lion pierces its prey with sharp, hollow jaws and sucks the juices out of its victim. Ant lions are found worldwide, most often in dry and sandy places.

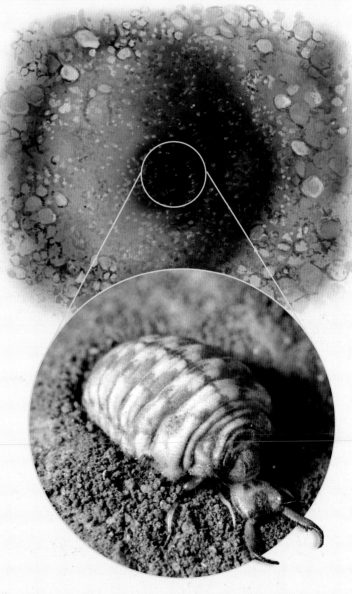

▲ *The ant lion larva awaits its victims in a small hole at the bottom of a pit a few inches across. Look for the pits in dry, sunny, sheltered spots, particularly on south-facing slopes.*

Cockroaches and Beetles

Most cockroaches live outside, but the kinds that live in buildings are the best known. Earwigs can be found in every backyard. Beetles are one of the largest groups of insects—there are more than a quarter of a million species known. They have strong mouthparts for chewing their food and two pairs of wings. The front pair are hard and act as covers for the more delicate back wings.

▲ Bark beetles have dug out "galleries" of holes in the bark of this tree. Each hole contains a beetle egg.

Common Earwig

SIZE Body: up to ¾ in (2 cm) long
RANGE Europe and North America
HABITAT Damp, dark places among grass, trees, and even inside buildings
FOOD Leaves, fruit, and flowers; also eats mites and insect larvae
TRACKS AND SIGNS These are some of the easiest insects to find. Lift a stone, plant pot, or log in a damp corner, and you are likely to see earwigs scurrying away.
COMMENTS The female earwig lays her eggs in a burrow and stays with them until a few days after they hatch.

European Stag Beetle

SIZE Body: up to 3 in (8 cm) long, but many other stag beetle species are smaller
RANGE Europe; many other species worldwide
HABITAT Woodland, especially in tropical areas
FOOD Adults eat tree sap and leaves; larvae feed on the juices of rotting wood
TRACKS AND SIGNS These insects, like their cousin the Giant Stag Beetle of North America, are easy to recognize because of their large size and the huge branching jaws of the male. You are most likely to spot them in the breeding season, when rival males battle each other to win females. A good place to look is anywhere there is dead or rotting wood.
COMMENTS If a stag beetle lands on its back during a fight, it is very difficult for it to right itself again and it may get snapped up by a bird or other predator.

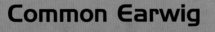

Diving Beetle

SIZE Body: up to 1½ in (4 cm) long
RANGE Many species worldwide
HABITAT Ponds, rivers, streams
FOOD Insect larvae, tadpoles, small fish
TRACKS AND SIGNS Look for these large beetles in ponds, using their back legs like oars to move through the water. You may see the larvae, too, which are fierce hunters. The pupae of these beetles are found in mud near the water.
COMMENTS You sometimes see these beetles flying out of the water at night. They are attracted to lights.

Stag Beetle Life Cycle

Female stag beetles usually lay their eggs in cracks in logs or dead tree stumps. The eggs hatch into wormlike larvae called grubs. As a larva feeds and grows, it sheds its skin several times and grows a new one. When the larva is fully grown, it becomes a pupa. Inside its case, the pupa does not feed while it changes into the adult form.

German Cockroach

SIZE Body: up to 1 in (2.5 cm) long
RANGE Now worldwide
HABITAT Houses, factories, restaurants
FOOD Anything eaten by people or other animals
TRACKS AND SIGNS These cockroaches leave a number of signs of their presence. Among them are little brown droppings, about the size of coffee grounds, and skins shed by young cockroaches as they grow. You may also find the little purse-shaped containers in which the female cockroach lays her eggs. She leaves this egg case in a dark safe place before the eggs hatch.
COMMENTS Cockroaches usually hide during the day and come out at night to find food.

▼ In very soft terrain, such as sand, beetles may leave tracks with their six legs. The tracks are quite similar from species to species, apart from their size.

▲ This female American Cockroach is carrying an egg case—the square-shaped object on the right—on her abdomen.

Bugs and Flies

The word "bug" is sometimes used for insects generally, but bugs are in fact a particular group of insects. These include stinkbugs, cicadas, froghoppers, aphids, and many other species. All have special mouthparts for piercing plants or other food and sucking out the juices. Flies are one of the biggest groups of insects. An important feature of flies is that they have only one pair of wings for flying, not two as many other insects do.

◄ *In springtime, look on leaves for stinkbug eggs like these. You may find other insects feeding on the eggs.*

Cicada

SIZE Body: up to 2 in (5 cm) long
RANGE Warm and tropical parts of the world (many different species)
HABITAT Forest, woodland, grassland
FOOD Young cicadas live underground and feed on the juice from tree roots; adults seldom eat
TRACKS AND SIGNS Young cicadas molt a number of times as they grow underground. You may find the empty skins from the final molt when the adult cicadas emerge.
COMMENTS Listen for the shrill call of the males. This is made by a pair of structures called tymbals on the body, which are vibrated by special muscles. The cicada's song is used to attract mates, and each of the thousands of species has its own song.

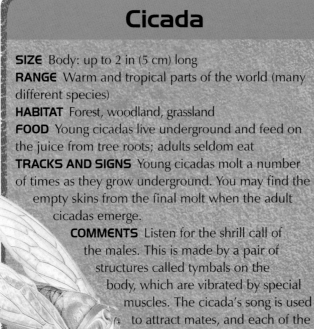

Froghopper or Spittlebug

SIZE Body: up to ½ in (1.2 cm)
RANGE Worldwide (many different species)
HABITAT Meadows, woodland edges
FOOD Adults eat tree sap and leaves; larvae feed on the juices of rotting wood
TRACKS AND SIGNS Adult froghoppers hop about on leaves as they feed, but you are most likely to see signs of the young, which are called nymphs. The nymphs cover themselves with bubbles of spit to keep them hidden from predators as they feed. You can see this frothy mass, sometimes called cuckoo spit, on plants.
COMMENTS These little bugs are champion jumpers. They can leap more than 100 times their own length up into the air.

Life Cycle of a Mosquito

A mosquito is a kind of fly. Mosquitoes lay their eggs in water or on aquatic plants. Some lay single eggs, others lay eggs in clumps called rafts. Single eggs are too small to see, but you may be able to spot rafts of eggs on the surface of a pond or in water in a container such as a birdbath or gutter. The eggs hatch into larvae, which hang just below the water surface and feed on tiny plants and animals (plankton). When fully grown, each larva makes a pupal case around itself and stops eating. A few days later, the pupa pops open at the water surface and the adult climbs out and flies away.

► *The mosquito's eggs hatch into larvae. Each larva becomes a pupa, which changes into the adult fly.*

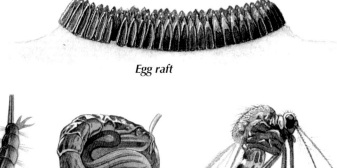

Egg raft

Pupa

Adult

Larva

Blowfly

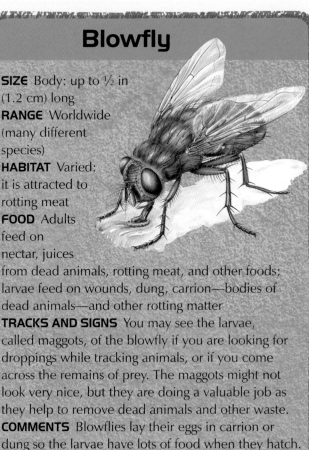

SIZE Body: up to ½ in (1.2 cm) long
RANGE Worldwide (many different species)
HABITAT Varied: it is attracted to rotting meat
FOOD Adults feed on nectar, juices from dead animals, rotting meat, and other foods; larvae feed on wounds, dung, carrion—bodies of dead animals—and other rotting matter
TRACKS AND SIGNS You may see the larvae, called maggots, of the blowfly if you are looking for droppings while tracking animals, or if you come across the remains of prey. The maggots might not look very nice, but they are doing a valuable job as they help to remove dead animals and other waste.
COMMENTS Blowflies lay their eggs in carrion or dung so the larvae have lots of food when they hatch.

▼ *The pink areas on this leaf are called galls—abnormal growths on plants that form around a newly laid insect egg or a hatched egg. A larva develops inside each gall and feeds on it. Look for galls on leaves, stems, and other parts of plants.*

Grasshoppers, Dragonflies, and Mantids

Grasshoppers are not very strong fliers, and they spend a good deal of time on the ground. They can leap into the air to escape from danger. Dragonflies are some of the fastest flying insects. A dragonfly spends the first part of its life as a water-living nymph. Mantids are some of the fiercest of all insect hunters. They have long front legs, which they can shoot out at top speed to catch prey.

▲ *This female grasshopper is depositing her eggs in the ground. The eggs hatch into miniature versions of the adult.*

Darner Dragonfly

SIZE Body: up to 3¼ in (8 cm) long; wingspan up to 4¼ in (11 cm)
RANGE North America (similar species worldwide)
HABITAT Near ponds and streams
FOOD Adults eat insects such as mosquitoes and midges. Young (called nymphs or naiads) eat tadpoles, water insects, and insect larvae.
TRACKS AND SIGNS Dragonflies can reach speeds of 55 mph (85 km/h). Watch for them darting back and forth with their legs held ready to seize prey. They lay eggs in or close to water. When fully grown, the nymphs crawl out of the water to transform into adults and you can sometimes find the discarded nymphal skin.
COMMENTS When at rest, a dragonfly holds its wings stretched out, not folded away.

Katydid

SIZE Body: up to 3 in (7.5 cm) long
RANGE Worldwide (more species in tropical areas)
HABITAT Fields, woodland, backyards
FOOD Leaves of deciduous trees and bushes
TRACKS AND SIGNS Many katydids are colored and shaped to look like leaves and even have markings like the veins of leaves. This makes them very difficult to spot as they sit feeding on the twigs of trees. You may hear their chirping call before you manage to spot the insects. Their call is said to sound like "katy-did," and that is how this insect gets its common name. Look for the long antennae too.
COMMENTS The female lays her eggs in plant stems. She cuts a slot using her egg-laying tube and then lays the eggs inside.

Praying Mantis

SIZE Body: up to 6 in (15 cm) long
RANGE Many species worldwide in warm and tropical areas
HABITAT Very varied—fields, backyards, rain forest
FOOD Insects, including moths, grasshoppers, flies
TRACKS AND SIGNS The many species of mantids are difficult to spot, as they are often colored to match the leaves or flowers they live among, to help them hide from their prey. Check flowering plants and watch for male mantids flying around outdoor lights.
COMMENTS If you do see a mantid, stay very still and observe its powerful front legs, which are its hunting tools. The legs are lined with sharp spines, which help the insect hold on to its struggling prey.

Short-horned Grasshopper

SIZE Body: up to 3¼ in (8 cm) long
RANGE Worldwide (many different species)
HABITAT Grassland, woods, sandy areas, rain forest
FOOD Leaves, grasses
TRACKS AND SIGNS Listen for the song, which these grasshoppers make by rubbing special areas of the back wings against the front wings. They may be difficult to spot, but if startled, this grasshopper can leap up to 200 times its own length.
COMMENTS Short-horned grasshoppers lay their eggs in the ground. The eggs hatch into young, which quickly develop into tiny versions of the adults. They molt five or six times as they grow to adult size.

▲ *Grasshoppers, mantids, and dragonflies are all nymphs at some point in their life cycle. They leave behind a dried skin when they transform into the next stage. This adult dragonfly is emerging from the skin of a nymph.*

Transformation

When a fully grown dragonfly nymph is ready to make its transformation into adult form, it crawls out of the water and up a plant stem. Its skin splits, and the head and thorax (first section of the body) come out. The legs and wings follow and then the abdomen (the long part of the body) emerges. The dragonfly waits until its wings and body are strong enough to fly, pumping fluid into the veins in its wings, then takes off, leaving its old skin behind on the plant stem.

Tracks Quiz

Can you guess which animals' tracks are shown on these pages? There are lots of clues to look for, such as the number of toes, whether or not claws are showing, and whether you think the feet look as though they can grip. To give you a start, the colors of the tracks match the boxes in the chapter the animals are found in. You can find the answers on page 192.

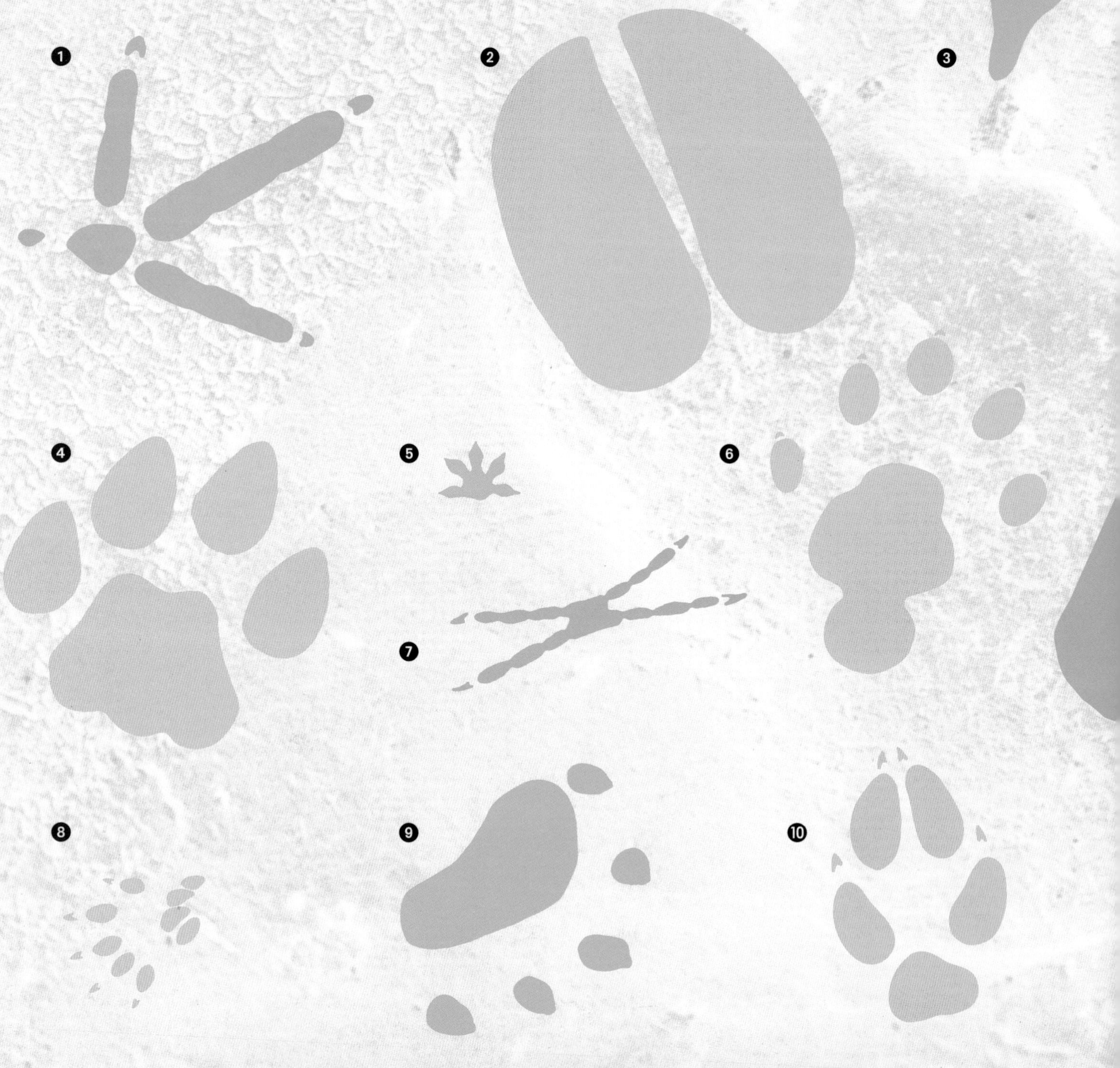

❶

❷

❸

❹

❺

❻

❼

❽

❾

❿

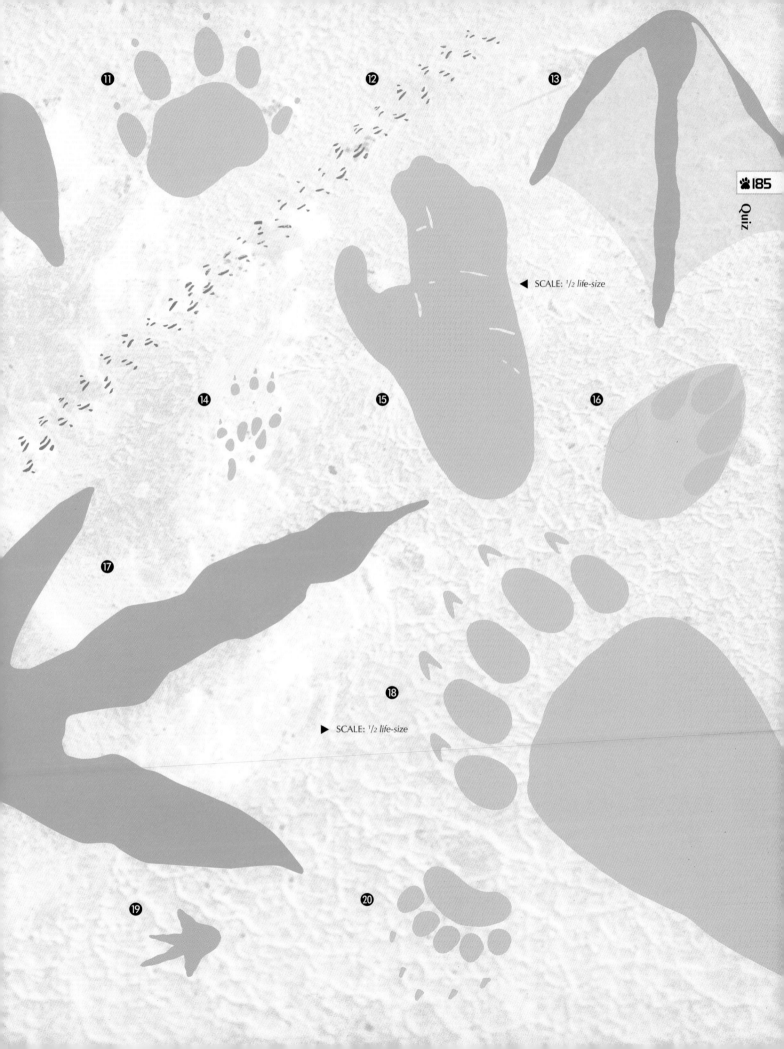

◀ SCALE: ¹/₂ *life-size*

▶ SCALE: ¹/₂ *life-size*

⑪

⑫

⑬

⑭

⑮

⑯

⑰

⑱

⑲

⑳

Glossary

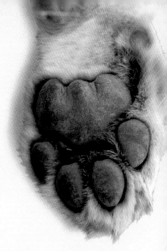

AMPHIBIAN
A cold-blooded animal that can live in both land and water. Amphibians include newts, salamanders, frogs, and toads.

ANTLERS
A pair of branching horns on the head of a deer, usually only the male. Antlers are made of solid bone covered with fine skin and short hairs. They are shed and regrown each year.

CAMOUFLAGE
The colors or patterns on an animal's body that help it blend in with its surroundings so it cannot easily be seen by enemies or prey.

CARNIVORE
An animal that eats other animals to survive.

CARRION
The bodies of animals that have died of natural causes or been killed by other animals.

CHRYSALIS
A dormant insect pupa, especially of a butterfly or moth.

CLEAVE
One part of a cloven, or split, hoof.

CLOVEN HOOF
The divided hoof of animals such as deer and cattle. The animal has two toes, which are covered with a tough horny covering, or hoof, split into two parts.

COCOON
A silky case spun by an insect larva to protect itself while in the pupal stage (*see* pupa).

COLONY
A group of individuals of a single species living together in one place. Many insects, such as ants and termites, live in colonies.

CRUSTACEAN
One of a group of invertebrate animals that includes crabs, shrimp, barnacles, and woodlice. Most have a tough outer shell. The majority of crustaceans live in the sea or in fresh water, but woodlice live on land.

DEWCLAW
A reduced toe positioned above an animal's other toes, which does not not touch the ground but sometimes shows in tracks, especially in snow or deep mud.

DIGITIGRADE
Describes an animal that walks on its toes.

DROPPINGS
An animal's feces (also known as scat).

GAIT
The way an animal is moving at a particular time. Walking, trotting, and galloping are examples of different gaits commonly found in mammals.

GLAND
A part of the body that produces special substances, such as saliva, poisons, and smelly secretions. A special gland in a snake, for example, produces venom.

HABITAT
The natural environment or home of an animal, plant, or any living organism.

HERBIVORE
An animal that eats plants.

HOOF
The thickened nail, or horny covering, at the tip of a toe bone on which an animal walks. Members of the horse family have a single hoof on each foot. Cattle have a cloven hoof (*see* above) that covers the tips of the third and fourth toes.

INCUBATION
The process of keeping eggs warm until they hatch.

INVERTEBRATE
An animal without a backbone. Insects and spiders, as well as creatures such as slugs, snails, crabs, and clams, are invertebrates.

LARVA
A young form of a creature, which hatches from an egg. A larva looks quite different from the adult animal. A caterpillar, for example, is the larva of a butterfly.

LATRINE
A place where an animal leaves its feces (droppings).

MAMMAL
A warm-blooded animal, usually four-legged and hairy, that gives birth to fully formed young. Female mammals feed their young on nourishing milk from their mammary glands.

MARSUPIAL
A mammal that produces young that are born in a very underdeveloped state. After birth, marsupial babies continue developing in a pouch on the mother's body.

MOLLUSK
An animal that belongs to the invertebrate group Mollusca, which includes clams, snails, and octopuses. They have a soft body and most have a hard external shell.

PAD
A fleshy underpart of an animal's foot; pads may show clearly in the animal's tracks.

PELLET
A clump of indigestible material, such as fur and feathers, brought up by birds.

PLANTIGRADE
Describes an animal that walks on the soles of its feet.

PREDATOR
An animal that hunts and kills other animals for food.

PREHENSILE
Describes a part of the body, usually a tail or limb, that can grasp things. Some monkeys have prehensile tails, which they use like a fifth limb to hold onto branches and other objects.

PREY
Creatures that are hunted and eaten by other animals.

PRIMATE
A member of the group of animals that includes monkeys, apes, and humans.

PUPA
The stage in the life of some insect species when they change from a larva into an adult. Butterflies, for example, undergo a pupal stage between caterpillar and fully formed butterfly.

RAIN FOREST
Forested areas near the equator, which are hotter and wetter than any other forests.

RAPTOR
A bird that hunts and kills other creatures, also known as a bird of prey. Eagles, hawks, and owls are all raptors.

REPTILE
A cold-blooded animal with scaly skin. Reptiles include turtles, crocodiles, snakes, and lizards.

RODENT
An animal in the group of mammals known as Rodentia, which includes rats, mice, and squirrels.

SAVANNA
Large expanses of tropical grassland with a few scattered trees and bushes.

SCAT
Another term for feces or droppings.

SCAVENGER
A creature that feeds on the remains of animals that have died naturally or been killed by other hunters.

SPECIES
A type of animal. Living things of the same species can mate and produce young that, in turn, are able to have young.

STRADDLE
The distance between the outermost edges of left and right tracks. It is measured straight across the direction followed by the animal, not diagonally (see page 14).

STRIDE
The distance from a point on one track to the same point on the next track made by the same foot (see page 14).

TERRITORY
The area where a mammal normally lives and feeds. Some mammals defend their territory fiercely.

TRACK
An animal's footprint.

TRAIL
A series of tracks or footprints.

VERTEBRATE
An animal with a backbone. Fish, amphibians, reptiles, birds, and mammals are all vertebrates.

WEBBED
Describes the foot of a water bird or mammal that has flaps of skin between each toe. The webbing makes the foot a more effective paddle for swimming.

Further Resources

BOOKS

Animal Tracks Guides series. Auburn: Lone Pine Publishing.

Elbroch, Mark, and Olaus J. Murie. *Peterson Field Guide to Animal Tracks*. Boston: Houghton Mifflin, 2005.

Elbroch, Mark, et al. *Bird Tracks and Sign: A Guide to North American Species*. Mechanicsburg, Pennsylvania: Stackpole Books, 2001.

Elbroch, Mark. *Mammal Tracks and Sign: A Guide to North American Species*. Mechanicsburg, Pennsylvania: Stackpole Books, 2003.

McGhee, Karen, and George McKay. *National Geographic Encyclopedia of Animals*. Washington, D.C.: National Geographic, 2006.

Rezendes, Paul. *Tracking and the Art of Seeing: How to Read Animal Tracks and Sign*. New York: HarperCollins, 1999.

Stall, Chris. *Animal Tracks of …* series. Seattle: The Mountaineers Books.

Stuart, Chris, and Tilda Stuart. *Field Guide to the Tracks and Signs of Southern and East African Wildlife*. Cape Town, South Africa: Struik New Holland Publishers, 2001.

ORGANIZATIONS AND ONLINE RESOURCES

There are lots of Web sites from which you can find out more information about the animal world, and many of these allow you to view images, ranging from spectacular photographs and videos taken by professional photographers to photos taken by amateur enthusiasts of all ages. Some of the best of these Web sites are listed below. If you have a particular interest in certain types of animals, you may also want to consider joining an organization that will keep you informed about them and will allow you to become involved in helping to protect them.

http://animaldiversity.ummz.umich.edu/site/
Animal Diversity Web (ADW) is an online encyclopedia of the natural history of animals at the University of Michigan. It contains thousands of accounts of individual animal species as well as information about animal classification.

http://www.arkive.org/
ARKive gathers together into one centralized digital library films, photographs, and audio recordings of the world's 16,000-plus species currently threatened with extinction. The database also provides profiles for many animals.

http://www.bbc.co.uk/nature/animals/
The BBC Web site Science and Nature: Animals offers many articles, images, and videos about wild animals and includes sections on planet Earth and conservation. The Wildfacts animal database provides profiles for many animals.

http://www.birds.cornell.edu/AllAboutBirds/
This Web site is an online field guide containing detailed accounts and images of many of the birds species of North America. It is run by the Cornell Laboratory of Ornithology at Cornell University, New York.

http://www.enature.com/home/
This Web site provides detailed online field guides for all the groups of wild animals and plants of the United States.

http://www.fws.gov/
The Web site of the U.S. Fish & Wildlife Service offers lots of information about identifying wildlife and preserving endangered species. It includes a multimedia section, from which you can download images from the natural world.

http://www.mnh.si.edu/mna/main.cfm
This Web site, developed by Smithsonian Institution's National Museum of Natural History, includes detailed descriptions, images, and distribution ranges for more than 400 mammals native to the North American continent.

http://www.nationalgeographic.com/
The National Geographic Society (NGS) is a nonprofit educational organization. On this Web site you can find links to a huge resource of various NGS media, such as magazines, articles, photographs, and video, including an online version of *National Geographic* magazine.

http://www.nps.gov/
The Web site of the United States National Parks Service is a huge site that offers a vast amount of information on the National Parks and wildlife of the United States.

http://www.rspb.org.uk/
The Web site of the Royal Society for the Protection of Birds offers many features, including descriptions of bird species and families, an online bird identifier for species in the United Kingdom, and many articles about birds around the U.K.

http://www.wildernessawareness.org/index.html
The Wilderness Awareness School is a nonprofit organization that offers online educational resources plus courses in wilderness skills, including animal tracking.

Index

Numbers in bold indicate pages where a more in-depth treatment is given to a subject.

Acknowledgments

The Publisher would like to thank the following for their kind permission to reproduce their images.

KEY

FLPA= Frank Lane Picture Agency
FLPA/HS = Frank Lane Picture Agency/Holt Studios
FLPA/MP = Frank Lane Picture Agency/Minden Pictures
MC = Magickcanoe.com (http://magickcanoe.com/)
N/PD = Nature/PhotoDisc
NPL = Nature Picture Library
NPS = National Park Service/Department of the Interior/Washington, D.C.
PL/OSF = Photo Library/Oxford Scientific Films
USDA/NRCS = United States Department of Agriculture/Natural Resources Conservation Service
USFWS = U.S. Fish and Wildlife Service/National Image Library

t = top, **b** = bottom, **c** = center, **r** = right, **l** = left

1 Tim Fitzharris/FLPA/MP; **2–3** Jim Brandenburg/FLPA/MP; **4–5** Heidi & Hans-Juergen Koch/FLPA/MP; **6–7** Thomas Mangelsen/FLPA/MP; **8** Tom and Pat Leeson/Ardea; **9t** Martin Harvey/NHPA; **9b** Roger Tidman/NHPA; **10t** Dave Watts/NHPA; **10b** N/PD; **12t** Jim Peaco/NPS; **12bl** Frank Balthis/NPS;**12br** Dennis Larson/USDA/NRCS; **13** Jim Peaco/NPS; **14** Danielle Jerry/USFWS; **16–17** Renee Lynn/Corbis; **18** Chris Harvey/Ardea; **20** Tim Fitzharris/FLPA/MP; **21** John Daniels/Ardea; **22** Dave Watts/NPL; **23** Mike Lane/NHPA; **24** Bev Wigney/MC; **25** PL/OSF Daniel Cox; **26t** NPL/Niall Benvie; **27** Norbert Wu/FLPA/MP; **28** Dave Watts/NPL; **29** Terry Whittaker/FLPA; **30cl** Mike J Thomas/FLPA; **30tl** Solvin Zankl/NPL; **32** Steve Hillebrand/USFWS; **33** FLPA/Sunset; **35t** David Hosking/FLPA; **35b** Andrew Cooper/NPL; **36** Martin Woike/FLPA/FotoNatura; **37** Brian Kenney/PL/OSF; **38** Hans D. Dossenbach/Ardea; **39** T. Kitchin & V. Hurst/NHPA; **40** Paul A. Souders/Corbis; **41** Wendy Dennis/FLPA; **42** Geoff Trinder/Ardea; **43tl** Simon Litten/FLPA; **43br** Jean Hall/FLPA/HS; **45** Igor Shpilenok/NPL; **46** ZSSD/FLPA/MP; **47** James Warwick/NHPA; **48** Chris Knights/Ardea; **49** Peter Davey/FLPA; **50** Cyril Ruopso/JH Editorial/FLPA/MP; **51** Ian Redmond/NPL; **52** Terry Whittaker/FLPA; **53** Anup Shah/NPL; **54** David Hosking/FLPA; **55t** Ingo Arndt/NPL; **55 inset** Ian Redmond; **56** Konrad Wothe/FLPA; **57** David Tipling/NPL; **58** Roger Tidman/FLPA; **60t** Jo Suderman/NPS; **60b** Richard Lake/NPS; **61l** N/PD; **61 inset** Jo Suderman/NPS; **61r** Mike Yochim/NPS; **62** Tony Heald/NPL; **64** Frans Lanting/FLPA; **66** Gerard Lacz/FLPA; **68–69** Andrew Parkinson/NPL; **70** Philippe Clement/NPL; **72** Ariadne Van Zandbergen/FLPA; **74t** J. Schmidt/NPS; **74b** PL/OSF; **76** Michael Quinton/FLPA/MP; **77** Angela Hampton/FLPA; **78** Tom & Pat Leeson/Ardea; **79** Nigel J. Dennis/NHPA; **80** Richard Anthony/HS/FLPA; **81** Martin Harvey/NHPA; **82** Mike Lane/FLPA/HS; **83** Richard Du Toit/NPL; **84** Brandon D. Cole/Corbis; **85** Paul Hobson/NPL; **86** Owen Newman/PL/OSF; **87** Alan Root/PL/OSF; **88** Adrian Davies/NPL; **89** Dembinsky Photo Ass./FLPA; **90cl** Laurie Campbell/NHPA; **90bl** George McCarthy/Corbis; **90tr** John Hawkins/FLPA; **92** Tom & Pat Leeson/Ardea; **93** Sumio Harada/FLPA/MP; **94** Jamie Harron/Corbis; **95** Stephen Dalton/NHPA; **96** Donna Dewhurst/USFWS; **98** Solvin Zankl/NPL; **99** Andrew Parkinson/NPL; **100** Simon Colmer/NPL; **101** Sunset/FLPA; **102cl** Bev Wigney/MC; **102br** Ed Austin/Herb Jones/NPS; **103** Rosalie La Rue/NPS; **104** Bev Wigney/MC; **105l** J. Schmidt/NPS; **105r** Elliot Neep/PL/OSF; **106** Francois Savigny/NPL; **107** Staffan Widstrand/NPL; **108** Gerard Lacz/FLPA; **110** Dave Watts/NPL; **111** Joe McDonald/Corbis; **112** Don Hitchcock; **113** Dave Watts/NPL; **114** Staffan Widstrand/Corbis; **115** Dave Watts/NHPA; **116–117** Theo Allofs/Corbis; **118** David Kjaer/NPL; **119** Bev Wigney/MC; **120** Malcolm Schuyl/FLPA; **121** Christian Ziegler/FLPA/MP; **122** M. Watson/Ardea; **124t, 124b** Heidi & Hans-Juergen Koch/FLPA/MP; **125t** Michael & Patricia Fogden/FLPA/MP; **125b** Steimer/ARCO/NPL; **126** Theo Allofs/Corbis; **127** Konrad Wothe/FLPA/MP; **128** Kennan Ward/Corbis; **129** Bev Wigney/MC; **130–131** Gary Vestal/Getty Images; **132** Mike Wilkes/NPL; **133** Philippe Clement/NPL; **134l** N/PD; **134rt** Greg Weiler/USFWS; **134rb** N/PD; **136** Mike Jones/FLPA; **137** Niall Benvie/NPL; **138** David Hosking/FLPA; **139** Tom Vezo/NPL; **140** Dietmar Nill/NPL; **141** Pete Oxford/FLPA/MP; **142l** Tony Wharton/FLPA; **142b** Jeff Foott/NPS; **144** Annie Poole/Corbis; **145** Jean E. Roche/NPL; **146** Fritz Polking/FLPA; **147** Dan Guravich/Corbis; **148** Brian Lightfoot/NPL; **149t** Don Smith/FLPA; **149b** Tupper Ansel Blake/USFWS; **151** Simon Hosking/FLPA; **152** Christian Jansky; **154** Roger Wilmshurst/FLPA; **155** Larry Michael/NPL; **156** Jim Clare/NPL; **157** Roger Wilmshurst/FLPA; **158bl** Roger Tidman/FLPA; **158–159** Dave Menke/USFWS; **159t** Jim Peaco/NPS; **159c** David Hosking/FLPA; **159b** Donna Dewhurst/USFWS; **160–161** Ingo Arndt/NPL; **162** Gary K. Smith/FLPA; **163** N/PD; **164** Stuart Westmorland/Corbis; **165** Matthew Perry/USFWS; **166** Bev Wigney/MC; **167** Geoff du Feu/Ardea; **169bl** Heidi & Hans-Juergen Koch/FLPA/MP; **169br** N/PD; **170** Bev Wigney/MC; **171t** Ian Rose/FLPA; **171b** N/PD; **172** MPFL/PA; **173** Fritz Polking/FLPA; **174** Kim Taylor/NPL; **177t** Ray Bird/FLPA; **177bl** NPL/Premaphotos; **177br** Jane Burton/NPL; **178** Myers/NPS; **179** Kim Taylor/NPL; **180, 181** Bev Wigney/MC; **182** MPictures/FLPA; **183** John Good/NPS; **186t** Fritz Polking/FLPA; **187c** Danielle Jerry/USFWS; **187b** Don Hitchcock

Answers to Tracks Quiz, pages 184–185: **1** Pheasant **2** Elk **3** Crocodile **4** Bobcat **5** Gecko **6** Otter **7** Woodpecker **8** Squirrel **9** Snapping Turtle **10** Fox **11** Tasmanian Devil **12** Beetle **13** Goose **14** Rat **15** Chimpanzee **16** Hare or rabbit **17** Emu **18** Grizzly Bear **19** Frog **20** Skunk